A
FULL-FIGURED
FAITH

THE EXPANDING EFFECTS OF DOUBT & SKEPTICISM ON AN EVOLVING JEWISH FAITH

RABBI PERRY RAPHAEL RANK

PERMISSIONS

Permission to quote from Michael Curtis' "Antisemitism:
The Baffling Obsession," as found in *Antisemitism in the
Contemporary World*, edited by Michael Curtis (Westview Press
/ Boulder and London, p.4), was granted by the author.

Permission to quote from Jonathan Sacks' "Not in My Name:
Confronting Religious Violence," as published by Schocken
Books, was granted by Penguin Random House, LLC, of which
Schocken is a division.

Permission to quote from David Rosenberg and Harold Bloom's
"The Book of J," as published by Vintage Books, a division of
Random House, was granted by Grove/Atlantic, Inc.

Print ISBN: 978-1-54398-481-1

eBook ISBN: 978-1-54398-482-8

To the greatest kids in the world, my grandchildren:

Nathan, Aiden, Ariana, and Meital

whom I pray will become both observant and thinking Jews.

TABLE OF CONTENTS

ACKNOWLEDGEMENTS

The list of those to whom I owe a great debt, along with appropriate reflections on how they have impacted on my life, would undoubtedly be a lengthy chapter itself, but there are those who deserve special recognition for the help offered in creating this book. At the same time, I acknowledge that any errors you may come across—grammatical, factual, or theological—are my own and will be corrected in any subsequent editions.

Rabbi Joel H. Meyers, Executive Vice-President Emeritus of the Rabbinical Assembly, has been an invaluable guide to me in professional matters and helped me navigate my multiple obligations to nevertheless bring this book to fruition. Rabbi Bradely Shavit Artson, who occupies the Abner and Roslyn Goldstine Dean's Chair of the Ziegler School of Rabbinic Studies in Los Angeles, California, was instrumental in reviewing some of the more technical aspects of the manuscript's theological musings. I am grateful to him for that contribution. His work in Process Theology has exerted a great influence in my evolving relationship with God. I am grateful to Professor Gary Simson, who holds the Macon Chair in Law at Mercer University, for setting me on the path of righteousness regarding some of the finer points of the law. Professor Simson has been a constant source of encouragement during the creation of this book, and I am fortunate to call him my teacher and my brother-in-law.

I first met Amy Gottlieb, my editor, through my work at the Rabbinical Assembly, where for many years she served as managing editor of the journal, Conservative Judaism. She is herself a master of the written word, both in fiction and poetry. A Full-Figured Faith has benefitted tremendously from her sharp eye and candid criticisms. It is said that editors serve as critics, therapists, friends, and Mommies to all the authors with whom they work, and Amy has certainly served me in most of those capacities.

A number of chapters within this book began as texts read aloud before classes I conducted at Midway Jewish Center in Syosset, Long Island, where I have served as senior rabbi since 1999. The good people who listened to those chapters would subsequently discuss the ideas and debate the issues, exchanges which sharpened my thinking and led to substantial revisions. I am indebted to their enthusiasm for learning, candor in reflections, and kindness in their criticisms. My tenure at Midway has been nothing shy of a blessing and it is largely due to the members whose commitment to Judaism is genuine. In addition, our community, myself included, is guided by a wonderful staff:

Joel Levenson, D.Min, Associate Rabbi

Ezra M. Finkelstein, Rabbi Emeritus

Adam Frei, Cantor

Lisa W. Stein, Religious School Director

Sandi Bettan, Early Childhood Director

Genea Moore, Executive Director

I owe an equal debt to the Midway Board of Trustees for granting me the sabbatical time so essential to the quiet, interruption-free periods needed for reviewing and re-reviewing that which will eventually make its way into a printed work. In particular, I thank the Executive Team whose members sacrifice their time for the greater good of the congregation and community, and who have appreciated my efforts in bringing this work to fruition:

Michael Kohler, President

Michael Schlank, Vice President

Tracy Slavsky, Vice President

Shari Senzer, Vice President

Brad Kolodny, Vice President

Mindy Edelman, Treasurer

Mark Abramowitz, Financial Secretary

Mason Salit, Chair of the Board

My father, Samuel N. Rank, passed on in 1983, and my mother, Hannah Rank, in 2009. I carry with me the lessons they imparted to me. So, too, my in-laws, Marvin and Mildred Simson. It is amazing how each could teach an entire Torah lesson in a moment, Marvin through his extraordinary candor and witty observations, and Mil by her ever-present and endless grace and generosity.

My children, Rami and Lauren, Shuli, Jonah and Raysh, have been a constant source of inspiration. I love the fact that they have pursued in life that which they love, all the while embracing their Jewish identities in their own unique ways. What they have taught me about fatherhood and parenting has shaped my theology and confirmed for me a rabbinic sentiment that the sources of wisdom are diverse and often surprising.

Finally, my deepest gratitude goes to my best friend, Ellen Joan Rank, an author, mentor, teacher, counsellor, rationalist, and curriculum artisan par excellence. She has gone through this manuscript several times and offered numerous suggestions for the improvement of the text. It is not often that I run sermons or articles by her, but this project was too important for her not to review. Of the thousands of decisions I have had to make in my lifetime, marrying her remains my best decision. And don't even get me started on her stuffed cabbage or cheese cake!

NOTE ON TRANSLITERATON

Words of Hebrew origin that have found their way into the common parlance follow the English orthography as determined in standard English dictionaries. Where the author has transliterated on his own, note the following conventions:

(chaf) = kh, like the "ch" sound in Chanukkah

(chet) = h̲, like the "ch" in Chanukkah

INTRODUCTION

One Friday evening, the Shabbat service ended as it typically did, with the singing of the hymn, *Yigdal.* There are any number of melodies for *Yigdal,* and that night, Cantor Frei, the cantor at Midway Jewish Center in Syosset, NY, chose an upbeat and cheerful melody. By the hymn's completion, the service had come to a successful conclusion, the worshipers rose from the pews, greeted one another, and made their way to the social hall for tea, coffee, and cookies. I was about to do the same when I was approached by Mel Morgenstein who asked, "Rabbi—when are we going to finally do away with *Yigdal?"* I was puzzled.

"Mel, what do you mean?"

"It's ridiculous. Half the statements in this prayer no one believes! If we're going to sing together, shouldn't we be singing about beliefs we hold to be true, and not beliefs that we have rejected?"

Mel, a man well into his eighties, who took his Judaism seriously and was intent on understanding the words of the prayer book, was questioning the relevance of a hymn penned over 700-years ago and that held a time-honored position in the prayer book. Mel was cordial and polite in his dialogue with others, forever open to understanding the particulars of

Jewish tradition, and very involved in synagogue. He even led a monthly discussion group on issues of Jewish significance. He was a thinker. And when Mel voiced a criticism, I listened.

"But Mel," I countered, "it's a happy tune and a traditional statement of faith. Do we have to believe everything we sing? Can't we just sing it as a long-standing tradition, even if we no longer accept each of its principles one hundred percent?"

Mel replied without a trace of conceit or irony, "No." He continued, "It's a prayer service, Rabbi. We should believe in the words we say and say the words we believe." He wasn't wrong.

One Shabbat morning, a woman and her daughter showed up at services. During the *kiddush*, they asked me why the Conservative prayer book was so different from what they were accustomed to in their Orthodox synagogue. I suggested that actually there weren't that many substantive differences, but that the Conservative prayer book was edited to reflect certain sentiments of a 21st century Judaism in order to be relevant to 21st century Jews. The woman asked for an example, as she questioned why anything within the prayer book would require an upgrade. I gave as an example the prayer about animal sacrifice. The prayer book of our synagogue included the ritual as a cherished memory of a past practice, unlike the Orthodox prayer book which called for its reinstitution in a rebuilt Jerusalem Temple. The woman and her daughter were indignant. "Our [Orthodox] prayer book would never have us pray to sacrifice animals!" At that point, it became clear that she was actually unfamiliar with what she was saying in her prayers.

Furthermore, it seemed as if she had comprehended the meaning of the Orthodox version of that prayer, she wouldn't have been too happy about it. For a person of faith, especially one who wants to pray with sincerity, knowledge of the prayer and some agreement with its sentiments ought to be key. One of the beautiful prayers of the siddur is "May the words of my mouth and the meditations of my heart be acceptable to You (i.e., God)." Yet before we request that the words of our mouths and the meditations of our hearts be acceptable to God, they ought to first be acceptable to us.

Yigdal is a hymn based on the "Thirteen Principles of Faith" as authored by Rambam, an acronym for one of the greatest Jewish philosophers and legalists of the 13th century, Rabbi Moses ben Maimon (1135-1204), also known simply as Maimonides. *Yigdal* itself was penned by Daniel ben Judah of Rome, around the year 1300. *Yigdal* is a synopsis of how Maimonides answered the ultimate questions of our lives. He sought to crystallize Jewish belief into a neat thirteen-point package. His thirteen principles of faith read as follows:

I believe with perfect faith that...

1. the Creator, blessed be His name, is the Author of and Guide for everything that has been created, and that He alone made, makes, and will make all things;

2. the Creator, blessed be His name, is one, and that there is no singularity in any manner like His, and that He alone is our God, who was, is and will be;

3. the Creator, blessed be His name, has no body, and that He is independent of all material properties, and that He has not any form whatsoever;

4. the Creator, blessed be His name, is the first and the last;

5. to the Creator, blessed be His name, and to Him alone, it is right to pray, and that it is not right to pray to anyone besides Him;

6. all the words of the prophets are true;

7. the prophecy of Moses our Teacher, may he rest in peace, was true and that he was the greatest of the prophets, both those that preceded and those that followed him;

8. the whole Torah, now in our possession, is the same that was given to Moses our Teacher, may his name be blessed;

9. this Torah is unchanging, and that there will be no other from the Creator, blessed be His name;

10. the Creator, blessed be His name, knows every deed and thought of humanity, as it is said, "The One who fashions the hearts of them all, who discerns all their doings;"[1]

11. the Creator, blessed be His name, rewards those who keep His commandments and punishes those who transgress them;

12. the messiah will come, and even though he tarries, I will be waiting for him the day of his arrival;

13. when it shall please the Creator, blessed be His name, that the dead shall return to life; may God's name and fame be exalted forever and ever.

These principles—not all but many—are the same ones that Mel was struggling with. Are all the words of the prophets true? Why must Moses be the greatest of all the prophets? Is

---

1   Psalm 33:15

the Torah forever unchanging, and if so, why don't we consult the local rabbis about our skin ailments, as the Torah directs? Does God really reward the righteous and punish the wicked? How does that synch with all we know about the prevalence of injustice and suffering? How can we wait for a messiah if we don't even believe in a messiah? Do moderns believe in the resurrection of the dead? Why must Judaism rest on these thirteen principles?

Maimonides would not be at all offended by these questions. He also dealt with a questioning Jewish community and sought to upgrade Jewish belief to fit with the prevailing philosophy of the day. Additionally, he knew that his thirteen principles were not above dispute. Jews have rarely been on the same page when it comes to defining the essence of Judaism. Maimonides was not the first to compose a statement of Jewish faith, or even the most ambitious. Some had sought to reduce Judaism to a single principle. For example, Hillel, the great sage of the early first century CE, famously said: "That which is hateful to you do not do to your neighbor. This is the whole of Torah. The rest is commentary. Go and study."[2] Fast forward about 150 years, and the famed Rabbi Akiba would declare the Torah's dictum, "Love your neighbor as yourself," a *klal gadol,* a major principle of Jewish tradition.[3] In this case, we need only strive to love our neighbors, and the details will naturally fall into place.

---

2   Shabbat 31a

3   Sifra, on Sefer Vayikra, Leviticus 19:18

Many have claimed Judaism to be a tradition of deed, not creed. There is a heaping spoonful of truth in that maxim. Jewish traditions are generally focused on doing, not dogma. Then again, the notion that Jewish tradition is without principles is completely spurious. There really is no case for belief in three gods, and we cannot observe the Sabbath on Wednesday, even if Saturday is inconvenient and Wednesday is a day off. So many questions! And often, the answers to these questions, emanating themselves from a vast and sacred and ancient literature, are themselves unsatisfying, particularly because we live in an age when religion is treated with more suspicion than veneration.

Judaism isn't the only religion with this problem. Many Christians are alienated from the traditional doctrines of the church. The denizens of western, liberal democracies are the heirs of the Enlightenment, a movement beginning in the 17th century that sought to elevate reason and science to a position the equal of or greater than the predominant ecclesiastical authority of the day, the Church. The proponents of the Enlightenment were hugely successful, primarily because their ideas worked. Their claim that over time, reason and science would generate greater gifts for humankind than religion ever did seemed to bear fruit. Between the 17th and 21st centuries, the advances in medicine, transportation, communication, agriculture, and mass production all combined to bring benefits to humanity that could only be the stuff of wild dreams in all of human history prior to the Enlightenment. Religious leaders naturally resented the attack on their authority and ideas, fulminating against the godless hawkers of reason over God's revelation. Their vindication of religion was more defensive than thoughtful or creative, yet in the end, even they could not deny the progress or the benefits that the Age of Reason (another name for the Enlightenment) bore. Religion took a beating, and on some levels, it was well-deserved. Nonetheless, it also became increasingly clear, over time, that reason and science were themselves limited, that effective though they were in advancing the material well-being of humanity, they had little to offer in terms of spiritual bounty. With religion having been humbled, that sense of divine purpose, the bold largesse of religion, had grown equally timid. Something was missing. It forced religious leaders to rethink how the ancient traditions could once again speak convincingly to a contemporary public. When so many people today sense a certain disenfranchisement from religion, it is due not so much to a deficit of information, as a deficit of inspiration. Rabbi Jonathan Sacks, an Orthodox rabbi, philosopher and theologian writes:

> Science, technology, the free market and the liberal democratic state have enabled us to reach unprecedented achievements in knowledge, freedom, life expectancy and affluence. They are among the greatest achievements of human civilisation and are to be defended and cherished. But they do not and cannot answer the three questions every reflective individual will ask at some time in his or

her life: Who am I? Why am I here? How then shall I live? These are questions to which the answer is prescriptive not descriptive, substantive not procedural. The result is that the twenty-first century has left us with a maximum of choice and a minimum of meaning.[4]

Yigdal is so named after the hymn's initial word, *Yigdal,* meaning "make great" or "exalt" and initiates the first of Rambam's principles with the words: "Exalt the living God." Not an unreasonable directive, especially for people who have a strong belief in God. Of course, for those who have their doubts, the exhortation to exalt God might be asking a bit much. How can they exalt a God they don't believe in? Can a Jew who doesn't believe in God continue to exalt at all? And how are we to understand that God whom we are asked to exalt? A modern-day *Yigdal,* updated to the sensibilities of a post-Holocaust, western, liberal, contemporary Jew, may sound a whole lot different from the one based on Maimonides' prescriptions.

Mel had unwittingly challenged me to define a set of principles that contemporary Jews could embrace. Over the years, any number of committed Jews have expressed their doubts and skepticism about what they know to be true about Judaism—the reality of God, the necessity of ritual, the mystery of miracles, the centrality of Israel, etc. These were not cynical people, iconoclasts, or rebels. They were not running away

4   Not in My Name, Rabbi Jonathan Sacks, Schocken Books, New York, 2015, p. 13

from their Jewishness. Like Mel, many were in synagogue week after week. In fact, these people were embracing Judaism, but one that was different from the Judaism of their youth. Their own doubts and skepticism compelled them to practice a Judaism that felt edgy and mildly heretical. They may have felt as if they had veered off the path of authentic Jewish living. They may have been told that they were not on the path at all, when in fact they were simply not walking as narrow a path as some would have preferred. Their Judaism may have felt edgy, but it was not at all heretical. Anyone who sincerely grapples with Jewish practice and belief is already squarely on the path, in spite of the protestations of all the "holier-than-thous" of the world.

This book is divided into thirteen chapters, each of which begins with a legitimate expression of skepticism. Each chapter ends with a suggestion for looking at faith in a more expansive way, or at least using a new lens to consider a traditional idea. Between the beginning and end of each chapter, I deliberate the complexities and nuances of that particular aspect of faith. One could conceivably rework *Yigdal* based on these deliberations, but the new hymn would not lend itself readily to a specific set of principles as it would to a broader range of religious faith that is accessible to contemporary Jews. I hope that each chapter inspires further discussion, and if it does not serve as the basis for a new *Yigdal,* I hope that I will have ultimately done justice to Mel's challenge.

1 THE GOD SKEPTIC

How can a rational person maintain belief in a God for whom no proof exists?

One day, the mother of one of the synagogue's pre-schoolers told me that her three-year-old got into the car after school and told her that God had visited the class. Pressing the toddler for a little more information, it turns out that God was balding and somewhat plump; he wore a knitted vest and sat on the floor with the other children. In other words, God looked a lot like me. At first, I was flattered. Then I was taken aback with the thought of how many other times I had created the conditions, however inadvertent, for these precious innocent souls to believe in a false god—namely myself. Finally, coming to my senses, I realized that this mini-heresy would be short-lived and there would be plenty of time to correct any other misimpressions or blatant acts of apostasy. In any event, the whole episode raised some interesting questions: How does one come to believe in God? And can moderns, burdened with several centuries worth of hard scientific facts, still believe?

My mother did not teach me to believe in God. She taught me to talk to God, twice a day, before I went to sleep and when I woke up each morning. I do this even now, though as an adult, I talk to God as part of a formal morning and evening service, usually at synagogue and sometimes at home. As a child, my practice was much more grounded in how our tradition scheduled this daily discourse with God, that is *"beshokh- bekha uvkumekha"* or "when you lie down and when you rise up."[5] That's how, as a child, I did it. I spoke to God right before I closed my eyes for sleep and spoke to God first thing after I had brushed my teeth in the early morning. I had no doubts about whether God existed. How could God not exist if each day I spoke to Him?! The reality of God was simply a given in our family, and certainly for me. There was no need to prove God's existence. God was already there.

I didn't have to think much about what to say to God either. My mother, again, told me what to say—the *Shema*, the Jewish declaration of faith: "Hear, O Israel! The Lord is our God, the Lord is One."[6] Even at that young age, I was a tad perplexed with the necessity of having to tell God something God probably already knew—there was only one God. But there was something strangely comforting in declaring that the "Lord is our God," a sort of affirmation that God was on our side, whether on the side of the Jews or the side of our family or just on my own personal side. I wasn't the kid who got picked

---

first to be on the softball team, but what did it matter? I was on God's team and God was on mine. That was one hell of a team. The team of teams!

In later years, when my academic courses delved into such areas as proofs of God's existence, I had to first assimilate the idea that there was a point to such an exercise. Why would there need to be proof of something so obvious as the existence of God? And thus I was introduced to people whose belief in God was (I almost shuddered to say it) tenuous, and others for whom belief in God was unquestionably a fallacy of human imagination. For them, there was no God. There never was a God. And just as all the gods of old—Zeus and Athena, Baal and Re—had been cast into the trash bin of vacuous and useless mythology, so too the God I spoke to daily was deserving of the same fate. Clearly, this was a world in which proof of God's existence was needed. Moderns require proof. But beyond my own conversations with God—really, monologues, in which I simply told God something God already knew—what could I possibly know about God, let alone prove God's existence? I had yet to meet with or hear from God and wasn't expecting to any time soon. And yet, I knew that I was going to have to search through the dusty tomes of ancient philosophers for some proof that God exists, if not for my sake, then for the sake of the doubters around me.

Unbeknownst to me at the time, this was not going to be a slam-dunk exercise. Hard proof was hard to come by. Aristotle (384-322 BCE), the great Greek philosopher, took a stab at the challenge. He looked at a world that was in motion—the planets, the stars, and the sun—and wondered what set all these things in motion. It seemed clear enough that given a sufficient force upon any object, that object would move, but then that force would itself have had to be set in motion. And there was the rub! The problem of force created a necessary regression, forever requiring earlier and earlier forces that triggered other forces that would put objects into motion. But could one seriously entertain a chain of regression that began earlier and earlier without end, or was there some beginning? Aristotle envisioned a beginning force to that endless regression, a First Mover, an Unmoved Mover that required no antecedent force. Indeed, this Unmoved Mover is what has become known as the Prime Mover. That Prime Mover is what others would have called God, though not necessarily the kind of God that our ancestors, the Hebrews, had in mind. Aristotle's argument is known as the Cosmological Argument. It's a wonderfully creative argument and very appealing. But it leaves some questions unanswered: Why must there be a Prime Mover to the exclusion of some other explanation for the motions of the universe? And even if there was a Prime Mover, how can we know that the Prime Mover is still in the moving business? Sensible as it was, the Cosmological Argument did not provide conclusive proof of God's existence.

Anselm of Canterbury (c. 1033-1109 CE) used the very human ability to think as the basis of his proof of God's existence. Anselm was a Benedictine monk and theologian, and at the time of his death, the Archbishop of Canterbury. Anselm believed that if you can think it, it must be real. He reasoned as follows. When a person entertains the thought of a tree, the thought itself is not the tree, but the thought points to an organic entity outside the human brain, with a trunk, and branches, and leaves, all of which together constitute a tree. That's how thinking works: what is first within the mind points to some external reality outside of the mind. In the same vein, it is possible to conceive of a perfect being, someone who is wholly good, kind, powerful, and so forth. Just about any normal mature brain can entertain such a thought. But to merely conceive of such a perfect being cannot itself be the perfect being. To the extent that we can think of a perfect being, Anslem argues, there must exist outside and independent of a human brain a perfect being. And there it is—proof of God. This proof is known as the Ontological Proof, ontology that field of study focused on being, becoming or existence. Again, it is a clever argument, but one that did suffer the blows of many philosophers' criticisms. One such battering came from a contemporary of Anselm, another Benedictine monk, Gaunilo of Marmoutiers (11th century). Gaunilo rightfully pointed out that Anselm's logic could be used to establish the existence of anything, simply by virtue of thinking it, like chimpanzees who play Mozart or penguins who prepare tax returns. Those are also thoughts that any of us can generate. The Ontological Proof was a powerful argument for those who wished to believe, but in the end, did not conclusively prove the existence of God.

William Paley (1743-1805), an English author and theologian, offered a proof of God from design. He asked us to imagine a stroll across a shore that involved the discovery of an abandoned watch in the sand. One might look at that watch and wonder how it got there. An examination of the watch would reveal a multitude of moving parts, springs, and gears, which of any other size or shape would render the watch completely useless. And yet all the parts are interdependent, coordinated, and purposeful. The watch, it would soon be determined, had a specific use and value—it measured the hour of the day. Paley argued that in pondering the universe, we see something akin to a watch abandoned on the shore, something that is of use and so intricately designed that no random chaotic set of actions could possibly have brought the elements together in so meaningful a composition. The intelligent design of so much of what is in this world, if not the world itself, points to a Designer, a cosmic watchmaker, who fashioned and crafted the raw materials into a glorious whole. This argument for the existence of God is known as a Teleological Argument, from the Greek *telos,* meaning "goal" or "purpose." The idea here is that an examination of this world, purposeful as it is, must lead to the irrefutable conclusion that there is an Intelligent Being who designed it. That Intelligent Being is God. The Teleological Argument, however, fell victim to the critics who questioned whether there actually was an order to the universe, or that the design of this universe could legitimately be defined as intelligent. One might certainly question the design of the earth—its abundance of bugs, its random shots of deadly lightening, its unpredictable earthquakes, its ruthless rule of the strongest at the expense of the weakest, etc. Could one say definitively that the world was designed for humans or could one cogently argue that humans came about accidentally, merely adapting to the world as best their poor biological selves could? The Teleological Argument was very powerful for those who saw order in the universe, but for those who challenged that very idea, the argument fell short of proving the existence of an Intelligent Designer. It did not constitute an irrefutable proof of God's existence, certainly not of a good God's existence.

For some, the absence of proof for God's existence was enough to convince them that there is no God. To be sure, no matter how many "proofs" are examined, they will almost always end the same way—interesting, creative, but inconclusive. And yet I knew, whatever it means to know, that even absent the proof, God nonetheless exists. And that is, I presume, the meaning of faith: the persistence of belief in the absence of proof. In other words, whenever we talk about God, what we do "know" rests not on tangible or verifiable evidence, the bedrock of what moderns have grown accustomed to in their unending pursuit of truth, but rather on people's faith and imagination. Faith and imagination, however, are powerful forces within the human heart. It would be imprudent to downplay either. They are both essential to life.

Take faith, for example. Everyone lives with faith. It may not be faith in God per se, but it is faith in the predictable nature of a world that allows us to act free of fear, despite the risks. Imagine a person incapable of driving a car for fear that such action will lead to an accident. In fact, driving a car may lead to an accident, but discounting extraordinary circumstances like inclement weather, a city full of drunk drivers, or faulty mechanics, the risks involved in driving one's car are so minimal that they should not impede anyone from taking the wheel. Reliance on that knowledge is a form of faith. The same is true for any who would dare fly or spend an afternoon in a busy city center or travel abroad. There is risk in virtually every activity, some activities riskier than others. Nonetheless, people press on based on faith that they will not become actors on the stage of the extraordinary or the improbable, and usually they don't. Without that sense of faith, life as we know it would be all but impossible.

Imagination is also an essential ingredient of living fully. It is the source of innovative problem solving; we draw upon our mental abilities to manifest a solution, an invention, or an idea. Imagination is not merely the domain of film, the stage, art museums or concert halls. Imagination is integral to such industries as computer sciences, pharmaceuticals, aeronautics, banking, engineering, and so forth. To deny this would be to ignore a basic fundamental of whom human beings are: dreamers. Imagination is as significant to theology as faith. There's nothing spurious about either. There is no overstating the importance of imagination or faith in living everyday life or in establishing the broad parameters of belief in God.

It's interesting to note that in all of the Torah's ruminations on God, relatively little ink is spent on creation. There are a couple of stories about creation at the beginning of the Bible, and then God as Creator is overshadowed by God as Guide or Master of Ethics. The idea that God would punish the wicked (would that He more often, relieving us all of that responsibility), redeem the oppressed, humble the arrogant, and care for those who live on the margins, makes for a tale that stands in stark contrast with the gods of the pagan world who operated capriciously, lustfully, selfishly, and with little or no regard for humanity. There is a reason why Israel's gift to the world is not merely monotheism, but ethical monotheism. The adjective "ethical" qualifies Jewish theology and suggests that this theology is not about the power and narcissism of a god, but about the justice and kindness of the only God there is. The Israelites imagined and placed their faith in a god totally different in nature from the others. They wanted a god whose very existence demanded a moral and ethical world in which both righteousness and compassion—the one not always compatible with the other—nevertheless interfaced in some sort of sacred tension.

Moreover, our ancestors asked for no proof of the existence of God, nor does the Bible offer any such proof. "In the beginning, God created the heaven and earth."[7] So the Bible begins—but who created God? No answer. And what proof is there that God exists? No proof is offered. God simply is. The

---

7   Genesis 1:1

unquestioned reality of God persists even today when those who make no habit of thinking about God's presence in their daily routines end up at some point invoking the name of God. Moderns are odd in that way. We study nature with no reference to God's involvement at all. Chemistry, biology, physics— these academic disciplines are taught devoid of any reference to God. And yet, a tornado that rips through a neighborhood or a hurricane that floods a community almost always raises questions about God or God's justice. In contrast, the courageous responses to tragedy, the first responders' heroism, the charitable organizations funding relief efforts, the relief organizations themselves offering help for no profit, the neighbors and friends who put their lives on the line for others—none of that gets attributed to God. Oddly enough, it is perhaps those very initiatives and efforts that most effectively create the presence of God. It is those gratuitous acts of kindness and sacrifice that allow for the presence of God to be most keenly felt. At times when it is most difficult to find God, it may be because people are just looking for God in all the wrong places, to put a twist on an old country song.

Menahem Mendel Morgensztern of Kotzk (1787-1859), also known simply as the Kotzker Rebbe, a Hasidic and Kabbalistic master, is said to have once asked his disciples where God could be found. They remained silent. And the Kotzker answered, "Wherever we let God in." The presence of God thus depends on one's presence of mind.

Once a year, a great number of Jews are drawn to the synagogue to begin the observance of Yom Kippur, the holiest holiday on the Jewish calendar. Yom Kippur is the Day of Atonement, a day devoted to cleansing oneself of sins accumulated during the past year. The ritual of the day is not all that difficult. As the day begins (according to the Jewish calendar, the day begins with sunset), one must refrain from food, liquids, bathing, sexual intimacy, leather shoes, and anointment. The day extends for some twenty-five hours, and those who take the prohibitions seriously begin the day with anxieties— Will I be able to fast all the way through? Will I be able to focus on all the prayers? Will I be able to start fresh and new, clear of sin? All these questions swirl around one's head as the day begins with the setting of the sun, the entire congregation standing, the Torah scrolls removed from the ark and held by various congregational leaders, the cantor intoning the words of *Kol Nidre,* the initial hymn of the Yom Kippur experience. It is a very solemn and spiritual moment, for those who understand.

A former congregant named Meryl hadn't been to synagogue in many months; in fact, she had left the synagogue altogether, but she contacted me in a moment of distress, asking to see me as soon as possible, if I could. Of course, I could! She came in and told me a story. She committed a terrible sin, possibly many sins, or so it seemed. She had been happily married to a man with a stable job, she was mother to three children who were conscientious and respectful, and they all lived in a suburban area of relative quiet and peace. And then it happened. She had an affair with another man. To make matters worse, the other man was her sister's husband. The plan was for the two to divorce their respective spouses and create a new and better life together. They were, after all, "in love." She divorced according to plan. Her sister's husband did not. He could not bring himself to lose what he already had. The whole affair went public and she had to face the ramifications: her husband, now her ex, hated her; her sister loathed her; her parents were angry with her; and her kids resented her. And the most unbearable thought of all—she suddenly found herself in terrible need of a God whom she hasn't really believed in for years. Her friends told her that she needed God. Her support group told her she needed God. Everyone was telling her that she needed God. But she wrote off God long ago. There was no proof of God's existence! And now that she needed God, how could she turn to a God that she rebuffed so long ago? She began to imagine the God that is, because it is through imagination that we begin to encounter a sense of God. And she then came to the disheartening conclusion that God must have rejected her too. Meryl sat in my office, weeping. And though she didn't quite verbalize it, she sounded only a hair's breadth away from suicide.

"Meryl, God doesn't hate you," I said.

"How do you know?"

"I know God doesn't hate you because God loves the broken-hearted. When a heart breaks, it creates the space for God to enter, and God, in part, is the energy of forgiveness." And then I told her the story of Yom Kippur, and how it really needs to be understood.

A lot of people assume it is enough to go to synagogue, stand, sit, stand, sit, mumble a few prayers, fast, think about the break-fast, schmooze with the Weintraubs, think about the rabbi's words (maybe), enjoy the choir, follow the cantor, and then, they think, they're good until next year. But that's not how it works. It works like this—

People sin. All people sin. Some people are aware of the fact that they have fallen short. Others are happily oblivious. But for those who know how deeply they have messed up, for those who feel it, for those who wear their sins like sand crusted upon one's body at the shore, they are the ones whom God forgives. But it takes standing before God and acknowledging that at every point in our life we are accountable to a power greater than ourselves that brings us the energy to go on. And God is always prepared to forgive. God is the energy of life, and the energy of life always seeks a way to advance, to move forward, to extricate the prisoners from their personal Egypts and lead them to freedom with the promise of entry into a new space. All that happens on Yom Kippur, but it can happen at any point when one is ready to face God. Any day can be a personal Yom Kippur. I suggested to Meryl that this day may be hers.

"How can God forgive me if my parents won't—or my sister, or my children?"

"They are going to have to answer to God in their own way, and God will deal with them," I responded. "In the meantime, you may be able to change their disposition by changing your own. Maybe not, but neither of us know that for sure. Today, you have to begin to live with the energy of God flowing within you. I have known you too long to think of you as an irredeemable reprobate. Face God and you will receive the forgiveness you need." She kissed me. She hugged me. She wept. She left.

Meryl's family has not yet forgiven her, but she lives with the faith that God has, and that has made the difference. For her, God is still not a fact, but God is something much more—a reality.

The story goes that when it came time for Oliver Cromwell (1599-1658), the Lord, Protector of England, a sort of non-royal head of state, to have his portrait done, he instructed the painter to create an image of him, "pimples, warts and everything," a known phrase often reduced to "warts and all."[8] There is actually no evidence that Cromwell ever uttered that combination of words, but the story itself is of interest. Cromwell was a religious man, and when he gazed upon his image, he wanted to see no deception, no alteration, no beautification. He wanted to see himself as he was. No more and no less. Our modern sensibilities would find that honesty appealing. And yet here is a paradox worth more than a few English schillings. The Bible, a document surely in favor of honesty, asks us not to see ourselves as we are, but to see ourselves as we might

---

8   Jack Malverne, "We've Been Looking at the Wrong 'Warts and All' Painting of Cromwell," *The Times*, November 18, 2013

be, as Anselm might have put it—wholly good, wholly pure, wholly righteous, wholly courageous. How is this even possible and how could the Bible make such a seemingly outrageous demand? It does so because the Bible insists that humans have been made in the image of God, and since God is the very source of goodness within the universe, our image ultimately should never be the image of what is, but only the image of what can be. To be created in the image of God is to be able to see within us the best of what it means to be human. To imagine goodness itself and have faith in the power of its materialization is to live as God would have us live. In order for people to live the very best versions of themselves, they have to have the faith that it is possible to do so. They have to have faith that God is.

Rabbi Dr. Reb Mimi Feigelson, the *Mashpiah Ruhanit* (Spiritual Mentor) of Jerusalem's Schechter Institute's Rabbinical School, once described an unusual Hasidic Sukkot service. She recalled an experience with a Hallel service, a part of the festival morning service, which in our own community is sung with much enthusiasm and lasts about twenty minutes, that ran over three hours. How could a twenty-minute service last for over three hours? She explained that it had to do with the waving of the lulav and etrog. The waves had to be performed with pure presence of mind and intentionality, something that the tradition refers to as *kavanah*. And so the Hasidim waved the lulav and etrog slowly, deliberately, mindfully, with deep and abiding *kavanah*. Those Hasidim were no more able to prove the existence of God than anyone else in the world. But their intent was not to prove the existence of God. Their intent only was to create the presence of God.

The people who create the presence of God, who are able to establish God as a reality if not a fact, do so on the faith that our lives are purposeful, that we are no mere accidents in the universe, and that we have a role to play in this world. The kindness of individuals who would sooner risk their lives to help a fellow in distress, those who would choose to pass up a neat profit if the transaction is morally compromised, those who are able to look into a world that is brimming with crime and corruption and yet find the goodness that exists, all these people are better than one thousand proofs of the existence of God. There are no absolute proofs of God. But there are people who because of who they are, and how they interface with others, are able to create a palpable sense of God. They serve as inspiration for the rest of us. If so inclined, we too can create that godly presence. The bottom line is a paradox. Even though we cannot prove God's existence, we can oddly enough create God's presence, and it is the creation of God's presence that is our most convincing proof that God exists.

And even a child can do it. How? A child does it not by some academic devotion to a proof of God's existence. A child does it simply by being instructed as follows: When you wake up in the morning, and before you go to sleep at night, you have to talk to God. Don't know what to say? Just say the *Shema*.

• • • • •

FOR THE GOD SKEPTIC

Strong belief in God is not childish and strong doubts about God are not heresy. The fact is that it is impossible to prove the existence of God. We may still, however, believe by living as the image of God. Through imagination and faith, it is possible to create the presence of God, the most assured way to establish that in spite of everything, God exists.

2 THE BIBLE SKEPTIC

*Did these tales really happen or are they
just folk tales?
And why do we continue to honor ancestors
who so often acted dishonorably?*

"Is this true?" people often ask me of that which is written in the Bible, to which I invariably reply, "Yes." "So it really happened?" is generally the follow-up question to which I generally reply, "Not necessarily." Did the Lord really create the universe in seven days? Did a group of Israelite slaves really cross a miraculously divided Red Sea to safety? Did those slaves then watch the same sea walls collapse upon their Egyptian pursuers? Did a prophet by the name of Elisha really lie over the body of a dead child and restore him to life? These are serious questions which prove that the reader is not simply dismissing these texts as fanciful, but nonetheless troubled by that which in any other book would be regarded as fiction. Could the Torah then be fiction? If it is, how could anyone sincerely regard it as the source of ultimate truth? These are big questions. And as much as I try to maintain the integrity of the

Bible, it does record stories that push the envelope of credulity to the breaking point. One of my favorites is a tale of a vile Nile.

Moses may have been on a mission to liberate the Israelites, but Pharaoh, the Egyptian king, was not keen on the plan. His recalcitrance was actually fortuitous because it allowed the God of Israel multiple opportunities to demonstrate superiority over Pharaoh, who was viewed among his own people as a living god. This is the backdrop for the Ten Plagues, the so-called "signs and wonders" that God would impose on Egypt to break Pharaoh's intransigence and convince Egypt that there was a king greater than Pharaoh. That greater king just happened to have been the king of those lowly Hebrews, the hard hats of Egypt's construction crews. Who knew! The Egyptians were about to find out. God instructs Moses and his brother Aaron to meet Pharaoh at the edge of the Nile for the first of the plagues. Moses tells Pharaoh that his refusal to liberate the Israelites has consequences. And Pharaoh is about to witness the first of these consequences. Aaron strikes the Nile with his rod and the river water turns to blood. All the water in Egypt, the canal and pond waters too, turn to blood. The drinkable water disappears. The stench of dead fish permeates the city. Is this credible?

It should come as a relief to know that a twenty-first century faith would never ask us to read these tales uncritically. That is to say, a contemporary faith would never demand that we suspend our reason while reading these texts. There can be no insistence on belief in a miracle that we know to be impossible. Did Joshua make the sun stand still? No. Not at all. Does that make the story false? Not really.

One day, while erecting my sukkah and standing on a step stool, I lost my balance and began to fall. My memory of the event remains with me as if it all happened yesterday. As soon as I lost my balance, a flood of thoughts rushed through my mind—mostly questions. Was I going to break any bones? Would I end up missing services at synagogue? Would I lose consciousness and if so, how long would I be lying on the floor of the sukkah? If I am disabled, who will finish putting up my sukkah? Am I going to die? How would people respond to an obituary entitled "Rabbi Dies in Sukkah"? I suspect that if any reporters from the local papers had witnessed the accident, they would have seen someone lose their balance and hit the floor of the sukkah all within a span of two seconds or less. But that was not my experience. I remember thinking how slowly the fall was taking and how many questions kept popping into my head. It was an accident that unfolded in slow motion.

I'm happy to report that I survived the fall and lived to write about it, with a take-away on the subjective nature of how we experience time. Two students sit in an auditorium listening to a lecture. One is interested in the subject matter; the other is not. One finds the time spent in the lecture hall to have flitted by quickly; the other, as if the day were moving at the speed of plate tectonics. Both students sat through a forty-five minute lecture, but for one the time flew by, and for the other time trudged uphill dragging a heavy load. Did Joshua make the sun stand still? No, but the memory of that battle was of a battle in which every second of warfare was felt and fully utilized. It was a hard battle and a battle that seemed to last forever, as if the sun itself suddenly hung motionless within the heavens above. Joshua made the sun stand still—a beautiful metaphor for the experience of a day that does not end. If there is beauty in truth, as there should be, then part of the truth of this tale lies in the beauty of its imagery.

Sacred texts are not designed to record history as we know it or conform to scientific principles. The expectation that they read like a scientific abstract or an historical account is to misunderstand their function or impose criteria upon this literature unfairly. It would be as silly to expect Indiana Jones to succumb to insect attacks, perilous falls, or hails of bullets. Who would want that? We revel in his ability to not only withstand such mishaps but to prevail over the bad guys, wielding his super-human talents in exploits of dazzling derring-do. Such adventure tales are not meant to reflect real events by real humans in real time. But through an author's talent to suspend our disbelief, a tale is told that surprises and entertains, and we would dare not demand of it any more than that. Sacred literature, in contrast, is meant to create a consciousness of possibility and miracle that at the same time conveys the shared values of an entire people. To expect that it do more than that is unfair. Sacred literature records memory and anticipates destiny, but to hold it to the standards of pure history or science places demands upon it that it was never meant to fulfill.

The miracles of sacred literature are not recorded to teach us that God is a magician. They are there to teach us truths about our lives and they do so in ways that are both fascinating and entertaining. Think of the expression "to curl up and die" or to "lock myself up in my room." These are expressions of withdrawal following a serious episode of embarrassment. The situation endured has been so humiliating, so debilitating and enervating that it just makes us want to curl up and die. The prophet Jonah found himself in one such situation. He faced a command of God that he could not bring himself to execute so he runs from God. He boards a ship that is soon beset by a terrible storm, tossing the ship to-and-fro upon a spiteful sea. The sailors fear for their lives and Jonah finally admits that he most likely is the progenitor of the storm as he chose to run away from God. The sailors must certainly have thought: Run away from God? He thought he could run away from God and actually succeed? What an idiot! And as for Jonah—how humiliating to know that the storm on the sea threatened the innocent lives of all on board due to his own cowardice. It was something that made him want to just curl up and die or be locked in his tent for days. And that is essentially what happened, but with a novelty that is gripping. Jonah is swallowed by a big fish, trapped in its belly for three days and thus freed from facing the people who knew just how foolish he was. Did a big fish really swallow Jonah? The best of scientific thought on this deems it all but impossible. Jonah's big fish story is a metaphor for what we all do when we need to withdraw and restore our confidence after a hurtful failure. Temporary withdrawal is not a terrible thing. It allows us to reassess our lives and regain the courage to return to life. And in Jonah's case, it defines the time needed to reestablish a connection with God. If ever there was a true fish tale, it's Jonah's. This biblical tale, read on the afternoon of Yom Kippur, the most sacred of Jewish holidays, is perfect for a day when we withdraw from the rest of the world to reassess our relationship and reestablish connections with God. That's a beautiful symbiosis between sacrament and story. And in that beauty lies a truth.

The sacred literature, it should be understood, is not simply one huge metaphor. That would be an oversimplification. Memory insists that we remember history, yet remember it selectively. Tucked away into the tales of miracles, laws, statutes and narratives are undoubtedly recollections of Jewish history. But history is not so much what happened, as much as it is how we know what happened really did happen. And in the case of history that stretches back over two millennia, substantiating what happened is not at all easy. The tools used to verify the historicity of a story, any story, are manifold—eyewitness reports, news reports, TV documentaries, literary sources, archaeological ruins, stoned inscriptions, coins, etc. These sources are not necessarily available to us when dealing with millennia-old events. Their absence does not mean that the event did not happen. It means only that we are unable to establish with certainty that it did. Insisting that the stories of the sacred literature did happen, as if that would be the only way they could possibly be true, devalues the significance of the messages conveyed. The morals of these stories are powerful statements of Jewish identity even if the stories themselves never happened. And the fact that the stories have made their way into a book that is regarded as holy means that the stories convey truths worthy of shaping our lives. Even if a specific sacred story was found to be a complete fabrication, it would still leave us with the question: What does such a story tell us about the people who crafted it? That's the kind of question that allows us to explore who we are today, based on a thoughtful consideration of the tales our ancestors told long ago.

No characters tell us more about who we are than the patriarchs and matriarchs themselves. They deserve special attention. In reading the Bible's narratives, the principle characters are all flawed, some deeply so. It is not uncommon for readers to wonder how it is that an Abraham could not protest God's command to sacrifice his son, or that Jacob could consent to deceive his blind father and thus capture a blessing that belonged to his brother, or that the greatest law-giver of the Jewish people, Moses, could murder a man and then flee for his life. The women in these early narratives fare no better. Eve, of course, was the first to sin by violating the one rule God had imposed upon her and her mate. Sarah insisted on banishing her handmaiden, Hagar, along with her child, Ishmael, who was no less Abraham's son than was Isaac. Though Jacob is blamed for deceiving his father, Rebecca was the brains behind the operation and therefore an accomplice. And Rachel lived much of her life consumed in envy of her sister, Leah. How can a religious tradition that espouses justice, honesty and peace be based on tales that so often record the opposite? And even more troubling, how have we found it possible to honor people who themselves failed to live up to the principles we hold dear?

In 2017, an article in the *New York Times* reported on multiple sexual harassment and assault charges against Harvey Weinstein, a major film executive, co-founder of Miramax and co-chairman of The Weinstein Company. The accusations were sufficiently serious and credible as to force his resignation from The Weinstein Company. Much of the film and theater industries distanced themselves, if not outright shunned him from their elite circles. What happened subsequently was nothing shy of a volcanic eruption of similar accusations by women who told their stories via the twitter feed, #MeToo. Within a matter of weeks, more film executives, actors, politicians, business executives were also accused as women felt empowered to tell stories they had kept silent for years, and in some cases, decades. The experiences shared were typically accounts of two parties of unequal power or status, the one greater than the other in which the greater wielded power abusively over the lesser. So though some of these disclosures were homosexual in nature, or of a woman subduing a man, the clear majority were reports of men taking advantage of or assaulting women. #MeToo seemed to serve as a vehicle of catharsis for so many women who had experienced such harassment, assault, and/ or rape.

The #MeToo explosion of 2017 followed on the heels of the decades-long sensational exposures of the predatory behaviors of the Catholic clergy. The revelation of one priest after another violating the trust of their parishioners, typically male teen parishioners, undermined the faith of many Catholics who had long suspected or kept silent about wrongdoing. It also confirmed the worst suspicions of any who long disdained hierarchical authority, especially that of organized religion. At the same time, questions percolated about those figures society chose to honor within the public square, largely dead white men whose legacy of great achievements hid the bigotry, hatred, and in some cases, murder, by which they were also known during their lifetimes. It seemed as if no one was spared publicity of their own shortcomings or sins. Everyone suddenly seemed flawed. Society discovered ethical failures from the revered actors in our historical consciousness to present day leaders in government, industry, entertainment, and religion. People are flawed, and that was the news, though in my own mind I asked: how could something so obvious be news?

Criticism of biblical characters for their shortcomings and failures has been noted in the commentaries for centuries, yet somehow their misdeeds were overlooked in favor of the good they did, and they are granted, within religious circles, honorifics befitting the righteous: *Avraham Avinu* or Abraham our Father; *Moshe Rabbeinu* or Moses our Teacher; and Elijah, a man responsible for the death of 450 prophets of Baal whom he slaughtered[9], *Eliyahu Zakhur LaTov*—"Eliyahu, May He Be Remembered For His Goodness." Should not these biblical characters be subject to the same critique by which the rest of the world is judged? Can an approach that favors the positive aspect of their lives be anything but a huge fraud or deception, designed to inspire within us reverence for characters worthy more of our disdain than admiration?

An answer to this question requires a quick trip to Paradise, or what the rabbis referred to as *PARDES*. *PARDES* is actually a Hebrew acronym which stands for four different ways of interpreting a text:

P stands for *p'shat,* the literal meaning of the text;

R stands for *remez*, or the deeper meaning of the text;

D stands for *d'rash*, or how a commentator may spin the text;

S stands for *sod*, or the secret meaning of the text.

These four approaches to the text exist only because for centuries, the Torah was never regarded as simply a historical narrative, or a treatise on law, but a book that guided the religiously sensitive to ever deeper levels of God-consciousness or meanings in their personal lives. The spiritually keen in every generation took to the written word in order to harvest its every allusion, mine and bring to light its secrets, and find within its ancient perspectives the guidance needed to meet new and sometimes uncomfortable realities. Over the centuries, their

---

9   See I Kings 18:20-40

discoveries and insights formed into what would become known as a *Torah Sheb'al Peh* or the Oral Torah. This was the Torah in which nothing was written, but everything was discussed, orally, between friends, teachers and students, husbands and wives. As long as the tradition remained oral, that is, unwritten, it remained fluid, organic and evolving. The Oral Torah would become so important that eventually the Written Torah could not be studied without first consulting the Oral Torah.

The Oral Torah looked at the characters in the written Torah and recognized them as family. These characters were not personalities of a distant past, but were the spiritual grandparents that had given birth to the Jewish nation. Were these characters perfect? No. Were these characters to be defined by the sins they committed? No. If what distinguished these characters were their shortcomings or their failures—in a word, their sins—that would have been the end of the moral and just civilization that the sages of our tradition hoped to create. Such a civilization could not rest on a founding family of thieves, cowards, and murderers. Above all, judging the ancestors harshly was not the way to treat family.

The life-sustaining dimension of family love for kith and kin is best illustrated with Seth's story. Seth was 26 years old, out-of-work, and very angry. As a teen, he was academically brilliant, athletically talented, and socially popular, but his dalliance with heroin turned poisonous and his life swirled in a downward spiral of deeper addiction and increased dysfunction. His unpredictability, inability to keep a job, and dangerous schemes for securing cash drained his parents and siblings of their patience and energy. Seth's parents were pained by their son's unfortunate turn, but remained unyielding in their hope that he would regain his footing. Eventually, he did. And though there was tough love involved in this turnaround, his parents never judged him a failure. They reminded him of who he really was and could once again become. Society might have written him off as another drug addict, as could his parents, except that's not who his parents were, and that's not how they conceived of a supportive family. In a supportive family, the good, the potential, the future, always takes precedence. A sin need not define one's life any more than failure—especially when it comes to the people we love. As for our biblical ancestors, it isn't hard to find within them redeeming traits. And the sages' sympathies for these characters' flawed humanity led them to that blessed redemption. The sages understood that to define the biblical characters by their sins, as if the only dimension of their lives was transgression, is hugely un-Jewish. It's not the way to treat family or ourselves in recognizing our own shortcomings and failures.

The tendency to identify our ancestors only by their faults belongs to a contemporary world in which the past is no longer revered, traditions are viewed with suspicion, and religion is a relic of the past that continues to disrupt rational living till this day. For those who may think of religion as a toxin, what better way to neutralize it than by attacking its founders?

But the sages of old were not interested in neutralizing Judaism. They were bent on using it to the betterment of society—and so they have, recognizing the sins of the ancestors without permitting those sins dominion over their character. Moses had left the comfort of Pharaoh's palace to see his brethren working in the fields. While there, he witnessed an Egyptian beating a Hebrew. "He turned this way and that and, seeing no one around, he struck down the Egyptian and buried him in the sand."[10] There is little question that by contemporary legal standards, this was an act of murder—deliberate, and judging from Moses' scanning the area for potential witnesses before he acted, pre-meditated. The "murderer" was well aware of his crime. The *p'shat,* the literal meaning of the text, is virtually undeniable. Moses is guilty and critics have condemned him as such. But as sacred literature which is meant to convey meaning—what is the takeaway? Certainly not license to murder our enemies.

I once had the privilege of listening to Rabbi Jonathan Sacks, the former Chief Rabbi of the United Kingdom, speak about what we learn from Moses the "murderer." Rabbi Sacks explained that the beating of this Hebrew was a crime in progress. Even if the Hebrew had himself committed some infraction, the beating punishment seemed well beyond reason, cruel and unusual. And so Moses looked this way and that, not to scan the area for witnesses, not to assure his own immunity from prosecution, but to look for some authority—just

---

10   Exodus 2:12

one!—who might stop this injustice once and for all. And as is all too often the case, there was no one. No one willing to step up and act with the moral authority that the moment required. It was then and only then that Moses responded. And here is the lesson: In a place where no one has the courage to act, we must have the courage to act ourselves. This is not a lesson in history. This is a lesson in morality. And it is a deep and abiding truth. If we were historians, we could at best let Moses wallow in a swamp of moral ambiguity. But for those looking to locate themselves within the chain of an unbroken ethical and spiritual tradition stretching back 3500 years, they must read these tales with an eye toward their spiritual messages—hidden deep within the text and waiting for someone to tease them out delicately and sympathetically.

In the holy Ark that the Israelites carried with them throughout their wanderings, there were two sets of tablets. There was the set we imagine when we think about the two tablets of the law, and the fragments of the original set that Moses had smashed when he witnessed the people celebrating around the Golden Calf. Why were the broken tablets kept in the Ark? Would they not have been better off discarded, as they were no longer of use? But no—their brokenness made them no less sacred. Like Elijah to whom we add the epithet, *Zakhur LaTov,* May He Be Remembered For His Goodness, we remember all our ancestors, broken as they were, with a sympathetic eye, not forgetting the good they wrought or the repentance they sought. If the Bible were only literature, a sympathetic read of its characters and events would be scandalous. But the Bible is not mere literature; it is sacred literature. These sacred texts are not easy to categorize. They are not books of science, nor are they books of pure history. They are best understood as a genre onto themselves. They are composite works of history, mystery, and fantasy. They are above all books of memory, the collective memory of a specific people. These books are a record of what the Jewish people have chosen to remember about our beginnings and our evolution, as well as speculation on our destiny and raison d'etre.

A good portion of this sacred text is devoted to one of the greatest tales of liberation ever told, the liberation of the Israelites from Egyptian slavery. It is a tale that has inspired countless generations of men and women whose circumstances have compelled them to cry out to God, from the American revolutionaries to the black slaves of the South to the civil rights activists of the 60's. The Bible serves as the foundation of a moral code for much of Western society, advancing the rights of the vulnerable—the blind, the hearing impaired, the widow, the orphan, the poor, the stranger, and though some may dispute it, women as well. The same text offers the reader a vision of the universe as portrayed as the handiwork of the Lord, a place which can only inspire awe and reverence given its magnitude, its complexity, its mysteries, and most importantly, its living beings. This sacred text is not a simple document. It is an admixture of the dated and the enduring, the horrifying and the uplifting, the incredible and the inspirational. How can something so uneven also be so holy?

By now we should know that truth resides not only in the domain of the written, but the domain of the oral. The holiness of the Bible oscillates between the written word and the oral examination of the written word. So when Moses and Aaron turn the water of the Nile into blood, they are not simply asking us to witness a miracle, they are asking us to consider the role the powerful play in damaging a society that should be full of life. By subjecting others, by beating the Israelites to do his will, by threatening their children with death, Pharaoh bullies the geographic veins of Egypt to flow not with life-giving water, but the blood of the innocents he has wounded and murdered. "Is this true?" people will ask me of this first plague, the water having turned into blood. I invariably reply, "Yes." "So it really happened?" Well, that's a different question. And as much as I love questions and regard all such questions as legitimate, it really is the wrong question. What makes the tale true is not whether it happened. What makes the tale true is whether we are sufficiently bold to let our lives be shaped by its message, in the case of the vile Nile, to confront the tyrants of the day with the blood they thoughtlessly spill.

• • • • •

FOR THE BIBLE SKEPTIC

We read the Bible's stories honestly and assess the lives of our ancestors sympathetically. We are not reading about distant characters of the past, but about family. Moreover, a literal reading is typically a misreading of the Bible. For centuries, the Oral Torah exposed the deeper meanings of the Written Torah. Oral Torah evolves even today, as contemporary Jews make these sacred stories their own by assimilating its messages into our lives and continuing to ponder the questions they raise.

3 THE WHO-REALLY-WROTE-THE-BIBLE SKEPTIC

What makes a book, clearly written by humans, holy?

Early on in life, I was taught in no uncertain terms that God wrote the Torah. At the time, it seemed entirely plausible because given all that God had to do on a daily basis—spinning the planets, feeding the animals, or listening to and sometimes answering all the prayers of millions of people around the world—writing a book was the most circumscribed of all the divine responsibilities. Why even question it?! And after all, since the Torah is not any book but a holy book, who other than God could have composed it? It was all very obvious until I studied biblical criticism in college and was challenged to deeply examine this so-called sacred book. Suddenly, it did not seem quite as well composed as I originally thought. It contains a number of repetitive stories. Stories do not always flow from one tale to the next. Some of the Hebrew is rather unintelligible. A few Aramaic phrases have been inexplicably thrown into the mix. Laws recorded in two or more sections sometimes contradict each other. Certain sections remain distinct from others due to content and language. In short, there are legalistic discrepancies and stylistic oddities all over this sacred masterpiece. Why would a single author compose a book with so many peculiarities? Moreover, if God was the author, and God presumably would be a better author than any other author in the universe, why is the Torah a work that would have kept a good editor busy for several months or years, as the case may be? It would be impossible to conclude that God, as an author, was only second-rate. Alternatively, if God was not the author, but the Torah was a work composed by the human hand, or possibly multiple human hands, could human genius alone actually produce a holy text?

The authorship of the Torah is no academic question. It is a question that has been a major focus of theological speculation since the Haskalah, the Jewish Enlightenment movement beginning in the 18th century. For those who thought of the Torah as sacred, holiness distilled into words, the notion that it possibly could be the product of human hands was blasphemous. And for those who thought the Torah was, like any other book, composed by human beings, the idea of authorship by God was sheer foolishness. Additionally, the implications of each group's position staked out who they were, more or less, religiously. A document authored by humans may certainly bear some errors, as error rests squarely within the domain of humankind. This school of thought would allow its members to more easily depart from the sacred text, knowing that humans authored it and get things wrong all the time. They could easily look at the Torah as the product of an ancient era, now dated, and thus be more open to religious reforms at odds with the Torah text. On the other hand, if the Torah was authored by God, then error in the text was inconceivable. Could God have misrepresented a story, omitting a needed detail or embellishing gratuitously? Could God have recorded a law mistakenly? Is anyone willing to ascribe error to God? The adherents to the God-authorship school of thought were less likely to see anything recorded in the Torah as out-of-date or flawed, for God's work must be eternal and irreproachable. This group would be loath to any religious reform that could be construed as a contradiction to the Torah text.

To be sure, over time, these groups generated scholars and clergy with more nuanced positions. For example, someone within the God-authorship camp might note that God may have dictated the words to a willing receptionist, like Moses, and if Moses misheard or got tired, perhaps there was room for some textual imperfection—due to humans, not God. Or someone within the human-authorship camp might claim that the Torah was nonetheless inspired by God, and the text therefore does retain a degree of sanctity—though ultimately humans wrote it. These were more nuanced approaches to how a sacred text could be the product of both God and humans, a somewhat relaxed position hovering between one extreme and another. But these positions are hampered by what seems to be a natural, widespread human resistance to nuance. Nuance happens to be mentally demanding and is thus so often lost on the majority.

Most of humanity operates with an either/or frame of mind, which is problematic to the extent that so much of life resists so neat a binary division. Politically, we may think of ourselves as conservative or liberal. Socially, we may be garrulous or guarded. Religiously, we may think of ourselves as believers or non-believers. Dichotomy is a way of keeping things simple without altogether suspending choice, but since it allows for only two choices, the menu is uniquely unimpressive. It's like living life with only two colors on the palette: red and yellow. One would hope for more colors in the painting and more choices in life.

Whenever I find myself in an Orthodox synagogue, especially an ultra-Orthodox synagogue, I am taken by those men who before prayer, tightly wrap a belt, sometimes referred to as a *gartel*, around their waist. They thus divide their body in half, isolating the lower part of their body with its attention to a person's animal functioning from the upper half with its focus on more intellectual or spiritual operations. For those who practice this ritual it is a sure way to create *kavanah,* or an intentionality meant to prepare one for prayer. But for those who might subject the practice to a more critical eye, one has to wonder—doesn't that upper half depend a great deal on the lower? Personally, I like the lower half of my body and say a prayer, now and then, in gratitude for its proper functioning. I don't think I would ever exchange the lower for the upper half, or vice versa. Logically, this dichotomy does make a whole lot of sense, as the two halves are dependent on one another. The ritual is well-intended and creates meaning for its practitioners. Nonetheless, dichotomies often operate as oversimplifications to an otherwise complicated and messy universe. And so, too, the question of biblical authorship is often reduced to an over-simplified binary choice. Either God wrote the Torah or didn't. And some would argue passionately that those are the only choices available as there is no third option. There can be no third option in a world which is dominated by either/or think-ing. And yet, historically, there were those who challenged and resisted this oversimplification. For Jews, it was Kabbalah, or Jewish mysticism, that offered a structured way of thinking about the messiness of the universe. By extension, Kabbalah may offer moderns a paradigm for how God and humans could conceivably collaborate in writing a book. All this requires a brief venture into the world of the mystics.

There are any number of Jewish mystical traditions, but the one that would address the issue of God and humans as co-authors would specifically be Lurianic Kabbalah, or the unique Kabbalah developed by Isaac ben Solomon Luria (1534-1572). Luria, commonly known as *Ha-Ari* or "the Lion," created a founding mythology designed to explain why things are the way they are and what Jews must do as part of their mission on earth. The mythology begins with the idea that God is every-thing. Forget about thinking of God as solely immaterial. In this theological schema God is the totality of everything, both the intangible and tangible worlds with which we are familiar. If God is everything, then there would be no room, literally no space, for something like a universe. God thus had to contract, that is, shrink in such a way as to create the space wherein the universe might then materialize. This Kabbalistic phenomenon is known as *tzimtzum,* Hebrew for "contraction." The vacuum thus created is essentially godless, which is a problem. Since some inkling of God, some presence of God-ness must inhere within the universe in order for life to take place, God then radiates God-light into this vacuum. The reference to God-light is not light per se, that is, the electro-magnetic energy of light as we know it, but a distinctly divine light, whatever that may be. This divine light should be familiar to us from the first chapter of Genesis when God creates light on the first day of creation, even though the sun, the stars, and the other celestial entities are not created until day four. This initial light, the light of Day One, is the divine light or energy that radiated into the universe in order for living things to eventually take shape. God's light did not arrive unpackaged. It was delivered to the universe in vessels. These vessels, or as they are referred to in the tradition, *keilim,* proved unequal to the task. They shattered due to the energy of the divine light and thus scattered fragments of divine light throughout the universe. This Kabbalistic phenomenon, known as *shevirat hakeilim*, the Shattering of the Vessels, explains why there is sin and sorrow, pain and distress within the world. The divine light which ought to be discrete, focused, and neatly packaged is scattered and diffused and thus serves as an explanation for the evil, the darkness that is so unavoidable in our lives, in short, the messiness of the universe. No one can escape this negativity; it is a function of broken spiritual energy. But as any good Jewish mythology would, a protocol is outlined for how to gather in the fragments and repair an otherwise damaged world.

The protocol is relatively simple. A Jew must observe *mitzvot*—divine commands, and there are 613 of them, as found in the Torah. It is through the observance of *mitzvot* and other mystical exercises that one goes about repairing a damaged world. This process is known as *tikkun olam,* literally "repairing the world." Lurianic *tikkun olam* has nothing to do with social action or liberal Jewish causes. It is a profoundly spiritual regimen in which a damaged world is repaired by gathering fragments of divine energy into a neatly packaged, pristine moment. How long will it take to gather all the scattered fragments of God's energy throughout the universe? It will take a long time. The universe is a big space and the divine energy is scattered throughout. A Jewish mystic's work is never done.

As with all mythologies, the Lurianic creation story need not be taken literally, even though for centuries kabbalists did and those devotees of the *Ari* today probably still do. Yet one needn't be a mystic to appreciate the truths that Lurianic Kabbalah points to. It posits the coterminous nature of godliness and godlessness. Within the same space of pain and suffering that humanity endures, there are people of good will who generously offer support and comfort to those in distress.

Life can be hell, but then there are angelic figures who popu-
late that hell, and just about everyone has met a few. The godlessness abounds in this world, but godliness is equally real.

A life of deception, greed, and selfishness is a choice, not
a fate. For those who would reject that choice, a life lived gra-
ciously, gratefully, generously, and mindfully is the contemporary version of gathering up those divine sparks. Maybe the
harvesting of divinity makes an otherwise godless world toler-
able, if not exquisitely beautiful. In any event, Lurianic Kabbalah
does not envision a world divided neatly between the holy and
the unholy. The holiness and unholiness are all over the place, a
confusion, a mess, a mishmash of joy and sorrow, righteousness
and sin. There is no either/or-ness in the Lurianic world. There
is, however, the possibility of grabbing a strand of holiness here
and a glittering of spirit there, weaving them together to create
a tiny fabric of shimmering goodness and God-ness. The Ari
would recognize that tiny piece of fabric as the end-result of a
mitzvah fulfilled.

Suppose, in place of shattered divine light, we envisioned
a random, arbitrary, and disordered array of colors, clay, musical notes, physical movements, or words. In the Kabbalistic
scheme of things, they could conceivably be thought of as
receptacles of broken shards of holiness as the shards of holiness are dispersed throughout the universe. Suppose an artist dared to reorder them into some compelling composition,
some ordered set of notes, or colors, or words. By way of example, take a random set of words: fire, tasted, perish, hate, great

and suffice. Most people would be hard pressed to find any connection between these words. Indeed, there would appear to be none, unless handed over to a poet, who might assemble them as such:

Some say the world will end in fire,

Some say in ice.

From what I've tasted of desire

I hold with those who favor fire.

But if it had to perish twice

I think I know enough of hate

To say that for destruction ice

Is also great

And would suffice.

Here the words of the great American poet, Robert Frost (1874-1963), are assembled in such a way as to create a poem, the total impact of which is far greater than the sum of its words. But the words themselves are not without power. They cannot be or else the poem would never work. The energy of the words, the shards of holiness are unlocked by Frost's brilliant repackaging of them. One might argue that the fragments of God's energy, dispersed as they were in a random set of English words, were gathered and reorganized in the hands of a gifted poet. There are countless other examples of this sort of divine repair work. this *tikkun olam.*

For years, my congregation, Midway Jewish Center, had an old spinet piano, discolored and cracked. Some of the keys were chipped, the hammer action was slow, and even after tuning the aged instrument, it remained the diva that had passed her prime. But it was great for simple songs like *Havah Nagilah*, accompanying the Religious School students during musical presentations or Chopsticks played by hundreds (thousands?) of teens who were at synagogue for youth group activities. One year the synagogue arranged for Rabbi Moshe Cotel (1943-2008), a composer-pianist, to present an evening of music and commentary. The good rabbi required a piano, and not just any piano, but a piano of quality and excellence, preferably a baby grand. The synagogue had no baby grand and the prospect of renting one for the evening proved as financially untenable as the spinet was untunable. When told of the condition of the synagogue's only piano, he hesitated only briefly before saying, "We'll make it work." The rabbi was undaunted, intent on giving this performance.

Rabbi Cotel arrived early that Saturday evening of the performance to inspect the piano. He examined it all around, lifted the hood to probe the hammers, tested the keys, and so forth, then remarked candidly, "She's almost dead." What happened that evening though was nothing short of a resurrection of the dead. Rabbi Cotel made the piano sing—sonatas, fugues, minuets—in a way that little piano had never sung before. After each piece, the rabbi petted the piano and virtually thanked it, asking it for just one more song, and the little spinet obliged. Somehow, in the hands of a Julliard graduate, a professional musician and spiritual leader, the latent tones of this pathetic instrument were marshalled together in a burst of musical elegance heretofore unimaginable, at least from that piano. It was as if the shards of holiness, this time tucked away in the music of Beethoven, Bach, Schumann, and Liszt, were brilliantly assembled and drawn out from beneath the hood of the spinet and into the social hall. Rabbi Cotel did that with music that had already been composed. Imagine the sacred craft of composers who draw original music out of shards of holiness permeating the ether, recording a note here, a rhythm there, crescendos and decrescendos, assigning each note the perfect instrument that would give sound to that note, assembling it all into some unified whole that could conceivably bring an audience to its feet, or to tears, or to both. Where did all that music come from? How do humans create something out of nothing? It takes a special person to draw the unorganized, isolated scattered notes, the scattered shards of God's light, into some intelligible and cohesive whole. It is a collaboration of the divine and the human.

In 1460 Florence, the Opera del Duomo, which was a sort of Works Commission associated with the gorgeous and imposing central shrine of the city, the cathedral typically referred to simply as Duomo, put a series of sculptors to work on Old Testament figures that would be positioned decoratively around the cathedral. Agostino de Duccio began work on one huge block of stone in 1464. It was a large piece of marble taken from the quarry of Carrara in Tuscany where the marble is among the whitest that can be secured. He roughed out some legs and some drapery but didn't get far into the project before abandoning it. Antonio Rossellino took on the project in 1475 and abandoned it as well. There was talk of too many *taroli* or imperfections in the stone itself. The block of stone which had been nicknamed "the Giant," due to its weight and dimensions, then remained in a courtyard for some twenty-five years before the Opera del Duomo fretted again about what to do with this stony eye-sore. Many florins had already been invested into it, not to mention the man-hours involved in transferring so huge a block from the quarry to Florence. After much consultation, yet another sculptor was given a chance to transform the Giant into a biblical figure. In 1501, at 26 years of age, Michelangelo di Lodovico Buonarroti Simoni, otherwise known simply as Michelangelo (1474-1564), started chipping away and three years later, presented the Duomo with an almost seventeen-foot, six-plus ton male nude rendering of a young David. It was a sculpture that would render Michelangelo's reputation as a master beyond question, an honor that remains with him until this day. What was it about Michelangelo that afforded him such vision, to see living, breathing character in stone, where others saw only imperfection and impossibility? If only Michelangelo were alive, the talk show hosts might have posed that question in an interview. Today, we can only speculate on Michelangelo's inspiration and wonder how much we ourselves miss of the divine, missing the scattered sparks of God's shattered vessels. Our blindness is alarming. The Kabbalists would console us and say: Search a little more, dig a little deeper, keep chipping away. It's all there. It's all over the place. Together with God, humans can create beauty.

Together with God, humans may even create holiness!

In 1990, Harold Bloom, professor of Humanities at Yale University and literary critic, wrote a book entitled, *The Book of J.* J, in this case, is an allusion to a popular theory of Torah composition promoted by the German biblical scholar, Julius Wellhausen (1844-1918). Noting the confusion of literary styles, subject matter, names for God and so forth in the Old Testament, Wellhausen developed and promoted the idea that the Bible was a composite work of at least four authors or schools identified as J, E, P, and D. D, for example, would be identified with the final book of the Torah or Deuteronomy. P, in contrast, would be a school or author that focused on priestly tasks and concerns, such as those richly found in the book of Leviticus. E is an author or school that typically refers to God as *Elohim,* whereas J is an author or school that typically refers to God with the four-lettered name, Yahweh, the "J" coming from the German letter used for the y sound. Of J Bloom writes: "...J is anything but a naïve writer; she is rather the most sophisticated of authors, as knowing as Shakespeare or Jane Austen."[11] In the course of this book, Bloom wrenches the words of J from their biblical context, separating the strains of J from the other authors, in order to recapture and restore its unified glory before some ancient redactors got their hands

---

11   Harold Bloom, David Rosenberg, *The Book of J* (New York: Grove Weidenfeld, 1990), p.12.

on it. Bloom sees within the Bible, within the words of J, a work of extraordinary literary achievement, on par or better than some of the greatest works of literature. J was a literary Michelangelo, a Jewish Shakespeare, and at least in Bloom's mind, a woman of extraordinary talent.

Bloom himself is neither a theologian nor a believer, so he would not ascribe to J any spiritual pretensions. But following our own line of reasoning, in which literary, musical and artistic works are a version of *tikkun olam* in its classical sense, then J was engaged in holy work, whether she realized it or not. But herein lies the problem. If J operated in the same way as do all gifted artists, and if the divine sparks within the universe are no more accessible to her than they are to any other artist, then what would render the work of J any holier than the work of a Moliere, Bach, or Picasso? Does not our updated, upgraded Kabbalistic theory of gathering the holy sparks, a sort of spiritualizing of the artistic process, not sanctify all sorts of achievements that have no place in the canon of Jewish sanctity?

It is true that so much of artistic achievement, even creativity that goes beyond the more recognized or traditional realms of art, can be understood as collaborations of God and humans—co-creators, in a word. But what makes a particular work sacred, particularly from a Jewish perspective, is a Jewish community recognizing it as such. And this recognition of the sacred expands with the generations. By the time the holy biblical canon was completed, the holy Talmud did not yet exist. By the time the holy Talmud was completed, the holy Zohar did not exist. And by the time the holy Zohar was completed, the State of Israel did not exist with its concurrent explosion of Jewish literary, musical, theatrical, choreographic and artistic expressions. Will this art ever be recognized as sacred? It is too soon to say. But the point here is that over time, the canon of the sacred expands. The Jewish spiritual canon is an organic body that continues to evolve. And whether talented artists have been able to recognize it or verbalize it, they have marshalled the shards of God's light that are fully around us, and created a holiness which is recognizable, impactful and inspirational. For this reason, it can be said that the Biblical, Talmudic and Kabbalistic literatures are all authored by both humanity and God. As Rabbi Bradley Shavit Artson, Dean of the Ziegler School of Rabbinic Studies in Los Angeles states, "The Torah is God's Word, but it is not God's words."[12]

One final thought on this human-godly symbiosis that makes for heaven on earth. There will always be those who resist the possibility of a human-God collaboration because they assume that no good can come from the hands of humanity, and certainly no perfection. These nay-sayers posit a supernal realm of godliness and perfection to which no human can possibly attain, and then another space where the rest of us reside, in an imperfect, difficult and troubled world. It's a conception of reality that suffers from the sin of oversimplification, a false dichotomy, the idea that there are only two options accessible to us. The dichotomy itself is contradicted

---

12   Bradley Shavit Artson, "Who are the Heretics?". American Jewish University website.

by the chanting of the Torah, a central feature of a Shabbat and Festival morning service, and a ritual which by definition combines the human and the divine. There are any number of ways in which the chanting of the Torah may be flawed, its reading considered not kosher and the listener blocked from fulfilling the mitzvah of hearing the Torah read. The Torah reading cannot be chanted from a printed text or by heart. This would be true even where the complete Torah reading is available in a printed text and recited by a member with flawless pronunciation. Not kosher. Or if a Torah is present, and the reader chants from the Torah perfectly, flawlessly, but by heart, the act falls short of fulfilling the mitzvah. It's not kosher. It is only where a Torah is available, and someone who knows how to chant it chants it directly from the parchment, that the mitzvah is fulfilled. But as anyone who has ever read Torah knows, the Torah scroll is a book of consonants without vowels or punctuation. It is, if chanted as written, a book of unintelligible divine sound. It is only when knowledgeable *Ba'alei Keriah,* those who know how to read the Torah, actually impose upon the text proper vocalization and punctuation that the text of the Torah becomes intelligible. That is because the reading of the Torah is always a partnership of God and humanity. So, too, the provenance of Torah is a shared authorship of God and humanity in which the shards of God's energy are reassembled and repackaged into an intelligible whole that continues to shine its light upon us today, and with the power to do so forever.

• • • • •

TO THE WHO-REALLY-WROTE-THE-BIBLE SKEPTIC:

To claim that God wrote the Bible may mean just that. But much of human creativity is a collaboration between the human and the divine. A sacred text, like the Bible, is sacred because the weight of Jewish sentiment over the generations recognizes within it a collaboration of the human and the divine. If God did not literally write the Bible, the power of the text exists as a testimony to a divine human collaboration.

4 THE REVELATION SKEPTIC

Science establishes truth. As for God delivering truth from a mountain top—really?

It's not easy putting God on trial, but it almost happened in July of 1925. This didn't happen in a secularized city of infidelity and impiety, but in Dayton, Tennessee, squarely located deep within the Bible Belt. The trial was officially known as State v. John Scopes, but it was more popularly known as the Monkey Trial, the name given it by H. L. Mencken (1880-1956), the American journalist and satirist, who kept America opening the newspapers with his biting coverage of the trial, his wit aimed largely at the prosecution.

The trial was a kind of mini-social explosion of an age that had been struggling with the interplay between science and religion. An increasing number of states had outlawed the teaching of evolution, a response to what was perceived as evolution's direct assault on Christian tradition, and more specifically on the biblical account of creation as recorded in Genesis. Tennessee was one such state. The Butler Act was a

Tennessee state law prohibiting the teaching of human evolution in any institution receiving state revenues. The American Civil Liberties Union (ACLU) wanted to test the constitutionality of such legislation and publicized its intent to defend anyone accused of violating the act. In the meantime, a group of locals in Dayton, Tennessee, noting the decline of their town over the years, thought that a trial of such stature could bring in badly needed revenue and put their little town on the map. Even the superintendent of Dayton's schools was in favor of the scheme. John Scopes, a general science teacher and part-time football coach who openly admitted to teaching evolution in the classroom, was solicited on the matter. He was willing to be prosecuted on the matter. The stage was thus set to challenge a law that gagged science and might simultaneously ensconce Dayton, Tennessee, population 1800, in the annals of history.

Putting together the legal teams for the prosecution and defense did not go as smoothly as intended. Eventually, two colorful personalities of the day found their way into the trial—William Jennings Bryan (1860-1925), the charismatic three-time Democratic presidential candidate and former Secretary of State, and Clarence Darrow, a prominent attorney who enjoyed a reputation for tackling high-profile cases. Bryan was known for advocating in favor of anti-evolution laws, viewing evolution as a direct attack on family and biblical values. Darrow, in contrast, was an agnostic whose work with the ACLU was well-known, and who was only too eager to take on a Bible-thumping populist like Bryan. Neither Bryan nor Darrow were the sole advocates on their respective legal teams, though their energy and passion fueled the dynamics of the proceedings. More than 200 newspaper reporters descended on this little southeastern town. Thousands of miles of telegraph wiring was set up to service all the messages that emanated from the trial daily. Coverage of the trial was front-page news in *The New York Times.*

The trial rose to a dramatic climax when Darrow asked that Bryan be put on the stand for questioning about the Bible. Against the advice of his fellow prosecutors, Bryan consented. Darrow questioned Bryan on those aspects of biblical literature that are most difficult to reconcile with, if not science, then simple reality: Jonah swallowed by "a whale;" a flood that destroyed the entire world; Joshua making the sun stand still; etc. Bryan maintained that though the Bible should be understood as written, there were those sections where a literal interpretation would be impossible. When the judge finally brought the exchange to a close, he ordered the testimony stricken from the record as it had no bearing on the case. The defense would eventually ask the jury to convict Scopes with hope that the case might be brought to a higher court where the constitutionality of an anti-evolution law could be addressed. In the end, Scopes was found guilty as charged and fined $100. The fine itself was overturned a year later on a technicality, but the conviction stood. It was not until 1968, in Epperson v. Arkansas, that the Supreme Court would hold an Arkansas statute prohibiting the teaching of evolution as violating the establishment clause of the First Amendment. Some states would still seek to circumvent the ruling by stipulating that creationism be taught alongside evolution as an alternate scientific explanation, but this tactic was also declared unconstitutional in Edwards v. Aguillard (1987), where the court ruled that the so-called "creation science" was an advancement of a particular religious belief and thus again a violation of the establishment clause of the First Amendment.

Science and God were not always at odds with one another. Many of the known scientists of the 17th and 18th centuries—Johannes Kepler, Galileo Galilei, Isaac Newton—were firm believers in God and the role God clearly played in nature. But the history of western civilization has not been kind to the understanding of God as Creator. Since the Enlightenment, beginning in the 18th century, God has been marginalized, and would eventually be excised from science. And so the scientific disciplines today are essentially devoid of any mention of God or God's involvement within the physical universe. In fact, Christian fundamentalist groups that have sought to combine God and science have met with a barrage of protest and argument, arguments that have framed those efforts as the product of ignorant, dim-witted, religious zealots. The attacks are vicious to the extreme, raising the possibility that there is more in these attacks than meets the eye. It's as if the possibility of a God who was in some way behind it all would thereby undermine the very foundations upon which some basic truths rest. All this presents serious challenges to a contemporary believer. Does God play any role in the natural world? Has God ever played a role in the natural world? What good is a God who cannot be understood as materially involved in our lives? Is the belief that God is involved in the running of the universe mere foolishness?

The idea that God may have created the universe in seven days (really only six since the seventh was a day off) is increasingly characterized by a sophisticated contemporary world as a myth, in the sense of something false and undeserving of serious consideration. This biblical myth runs counter to the scientific idea that the earth has been around for some 4.5 billion years and the universe for some 12-14 billion years. A further challenge to the biblical myth is the scientific theory that human life has occupied earth for a few million years, a fraction of the earth's actual age but millions of years earlier than the biblical narrative imagines. In short, the idea that it took God but a few days to create and put the universe all together becomes, within the contemporary western mind, laughable. The biblical story is further derided due to its identification of divine verbal decree as the trigger of all initial creativity. All of those "Let there be's" in the first chapter of the Bible constitute the stuff of fairy tales, not true science. And, of course, the ultimate criticism would be the presumption of a God in the first place. If it is possible to explain the existence of the universe without some divine agency at work, then it should be explained as such, and scientific theories dare do just that.

In a pre-scientific world, which would constitute the bulk of human history, questions about the nature of human life or the physical world were addressed largely through thoughtful observation. The idea that the sun rises and the sun sets is based on an observation. That ought to make it true but as it turned out, the observation was rather deceptive. Whatever looks like the sun rising or setting is neither, but it took thousands of years for humanity to propose that the motion of our most beloved and closest star may actually be due to an earth that rotates rather than a star that orbits. Such theories were bandied about as early as ancient Greece, but Aristotle (384-322 BCE), the great Greek philosopher whose writings about the physical world held sway for more than a thousand years, criticized that theory as counter to observable fact. Aristotle, mistaken as he was, was on to something very modern: truth ought to be based on what is observable, for only the observable is verifiable. Aristotle almost had it right, but didn't know then what we know now: what is seen isn't always what is. That turned out to be one of the more eye-opening milestones in the evolution of epistemology, or the study of how we know what we know. Still, the close association between observation and reality has been integral to the human pursuit of truth for centuries, stretching back to the very beginnings of recorded human history.

The power of observation was not lost on the ancient Israelites: "...Israel *saw* the Egyptians dead on the shore of the sea. And when Israel *saw* the awesome power which the Lord wielded against the Egyptians, the people feared the Lord..."[13] [italics are the author's]. And so Israelite faith too was in part based on observation. The Israelites saw something, they understood it as an act of divine salvation, and their faith was thus established. And yet, believing Jews throughout the centuries would claim that the truth of the Torah does not rest on what is observable, but rather on what has been revealed. The truth of Torah rested on the idea that God revealed it all to Moses and to the ancient Israelites. This is the doctrine of Revelation, meaning that what we know to be true is true because a good God revealed it to us. And even if that good God did not reveal it to us directly, we have a record of that revelation in the words of Torah. The Revelation began at Sinai, which initiated an unbroken chain of tradition that continues to inspire and inform us, generations hence. This is the point of the first *mishnah* in the rabbinic work, Pirkei Avot, that outlines a transmission of traditions that "Moses received from Sinai" and which subsequent generations passed from one generation to the next, right down to "the Men of the Great Assembly,"[14] of whom we know very little. The rabbis who conceived of this perfect and uninterrupted chain of transmission may have had some vague consciousness of legal historical developments over time, unrelated to Revelation, but they were incidental. The traditions and laws that were in the hands of the "Men of the Great Assembly," and by extension, in our very hands today,

---

13   Exodus 14:30-31

14   Pirkei Avot 1:1

began with God who placed them into the hands of Moses. Six days of creation, never mixing meat and dairy, resting once every seven days, leaving the earth fallow periodically—all of this was true because all of it was revealed to be true. And the Revelation itself, manifest most dramatically in the giving of the Ten Commandments at Mount Sinai amid thunder, lightning, smoke, and a quaking landscape, was evidence of God's love for the Israelites and ultimately for all the Jewish people through time.

This is a *weltanschauung* completely at odds with the scientific community, and with the zeitgeist of the contemporary world that has placed its trust in scientific method. Science generally reaches conclusions about the nature of the universe under the assumption that either there is no God, or for those scientists who are believers, that God may play no role in scientific theory or mathematical formulae. Believing scientists are a good metaphor for the predicament of all contemporary believing Jews. On the one hand, there is a powerful sense that science, which cannot permit any divine agency within the universe, represents a legitimate and extraordinarily productive technique in advancing the welfare of humanity—from medical to technological advancements. On the other hand, believers will be loath to think of God as inert or altogether absent within the operations of the universe. These two positions create a great deal of cognitive tension and compel people to choose one position over the other. But this polarization is not inevitable, for there is another path open to a modern believer.

Believers will always tend to defend and embrace the truths of Torah. But what exactly is Torah? Ironically, nowhere in the Torah does the Torah refer to itself as "the Torah." When used, the term simply means "teaching." Torah, commonly used in the sense of the Five Books of Moses, is a name given to it well after the Torah's compilation. The expansion of the term does not end there. Prior to the study of any Talmudic or Midrashic work, a blessing is recited in which God is praised for "commanding us to get busy with words of Torah." How is such a blessing appropriate when the object of one's study is not, strictly speaking, the words of Torah, but post-biblical litera-ture, like Mishnah, Gemara, Midrash, or rabbinic responsa? And yet, these various genres of sacred literature are referred to as Torah. To study any of these various works is a sacred under-taking and is referred to as the mitzvah of *Talmud Torah*, or Torah study. The intent here seems clear enough. Whenever a person is engaged in that type of study that moves one closer to God, or truth, or a deeper understanding of the universe, then that enterprise would be regarded as an exercise in Torah study. So Torah, which originally meant to convey only a spe-cific teaching, later evolved to encompass the Five Books of Moses, then came to identify the Bible as a whole, later to all of rabbinic literature, and finally to any of the discussions that would derive from those studies. In short, what Torah refers to has expanded tremendously over time. But could the term continue to embrace disciplines beyond rabbinic literature?

When the Ark is opened on a Shabbat morning in preparation to read the Torah, a passage from the Zohar, the mystical 13th century primary Kabbalistic text, is recited. This Aramaic passage is typically referred to as *Berikh Shemei*, or "Praised is [God's] Name..." It is a simple, lovely prayer asking for God's light at a propitious time, that is, when the Ark of the holy Torah is opened, a sort of earthly parallel to the opened gates of heaven. This is a time when one's prayers may most easily penetrate the firmament and reach God. In this passage, there is a section that declares the Torah and the prophets to be true; that is, all their words are true. But an equally legitimate translation of that passage alters the meaning ever so slightly, translating the Aramaic term *keshot* not as an adjective, "true," but as a noun, "truth." In that case, what the prayer says is this: "Not in humanity do I trust, nor on any angel do I rely, but on the God of heaven who is the God of truth, whose Torah is truth, whose prophets are truth, and who abounds in acts of goodness and truth." Translating the Aramaic *keshot* as truth now gives the reader/pray-er an important insight into what a fully expanded definition of Torah could be: Truth. Every truth is a Godly teaching. Every truth is itself a prophet of God.

The implication of such a translation is far-reaching, literally, as it would remove the boundary between the truths of sacred and secular study. Truth is truth. One of the Kabbalistic traditions of the morning prayers would have the worshiper conclude the *Shema* with the first word of the following paragraph, thus formulating a three-word declaration: *Adonai*

Eloheikhem Emet—the Lord your God is Truth. Truth and God are deeply connected, if not identical, in Jewish thought.

In 1687, a rather irascible and ill-tempered English mathematician and physicist by the name of Isaac Newton (1643-1727) instituted a revolution in physics with his publication of *Philosophiae Naturalis Principia Mathematica (Mathematical Principles of Natural Philosophy),* most often known simply as *Principia.* In that work he recorded three laws of physics, subsequently known as Newton's Three Laws of Motion, which almost every high school student in a science class is exposed to. They are, simply put:

1. A body at rest remains at rest unless acted upon by some external force;
2. Force is equal to mass times acceleration;
3. For every action, there is an equal and opposite reaction.

There is really only one function to these laws and that is to definitively describe how objects move, or alternatively, rest, within space. The rules as recorded above are rather plain in dress, but even in their more sophisticated attire they are hugely elegant in their simplicity. In just a few words, they capture the essence of motion and even give us the equations that would define motion numerically. No one would deny the truth of Newton's laws. That said, are Newton's laws of motion sacred? Are they Torah?

If God does not figure into your understanding of the universe, then these laws may be described as beautiful and lovely, but they could not be described as sacred. But if we do believe that God is part of the universe and that God is the Creator of this universe, then what Newton has done is more than amazing for the physicists of the academic world. Newton has exposed to the human eye a corner of a blueprint of the universe itself and allowed us to peer into the mind of God. If these laws are true, and if truth is Godly, then these truths must constitute a form of sacred knowledge.

Even if the definition of Torah were expanded to include all of scientific truth, does this not constitute a major shift away from Revelation, replacing it with Discovery? Will this not compel us ultimately to subject the Torah to a more rigorous critique admitting as true only that which is demonstrable, verifiable, or in a word, "observable"?

To be sure, the advent of Discovery has already made its mark on Revelation. That section of the Torah that deals with skin ailments (Leviticus 13-14) and the ways in which the priests would address those ailments has long been understood as ineffective. The remission of all debts in the seventh year, a result of the *Shemitah* or Sabbatical year (Deuteronomy 15:1-2), proved untenable for debtors and creditors alike—creditors, for fear of losing what was duly owed them and debtors, who had an increasingly tough time securing a loan in years five or six of the Sabbatical cycle. It was the great sage Hillel who created the *prozbul*, an instrument by which debt could be carried from one sabbatical cycle to the other without bypassing the Torah per se, though its practical effect was to do just that. Finally, the prohibition against charging interest to one's fellow Jew[15] proved to be a boulder's worth of drag on business advancement, again for both the creditor and debtor. At some point beginning as early as the 12th century, a *heter iska* or a contract that permitted exactly what the Torah forbade came into vogue, again without violating the Torah overtly, but whose design clearly circumvented an otherwise unworkable provision of the Torah. The Revelation may have told Jews what to do, but it was Discovery that told Jews whether what they were to do was doable.

These are all examples of how Discovery in some way modified, and in other ways completely uprooted, the Revealed Word of God. Ever since Sinai, the Revealed Word was always subjected to further analysis by scholars and teachers who worked their magic on texts they found difficult. That was, perhaps, the entire purpose of the Oral Torah: to fill in the blanks, to soften the intent, or to rein in the natural ramifications of a particular ruling. But once the law or tradition was actually modified, reined-in, subverted, or neutralized, the result was never regarded as a bastardization of God's will, but rather its elucidation. Discovery, as such, was never viewed as undermining Revelation as much as enhancing it, and the process continues, orally, to this day, as each generation struggles to understand truth.

Which values of the Torah deserve to enter the pantheon of ultimate truth? The answer should be obvious—all of them.

---

15   See Leviticus 25:35-38

But it's never quite as easy as that. Take a value as uncontroversial as honoring one's parents. It would seem like a value without even the possibility of reservation. Yet nothing could be further from the truth. Must a child honor a parent who is verbally, physically, or sexually abusive? What then does the abused child owe the parent in terms of honor? And given all the variations on the history of an abusive relationship, could there even be one answer to that question? The value of honoring one's parents is one that is certainly rooted squarely within the Torah's Ten Commandments, but under certain circumstances, it too will be subjected to heartfelt and sometimes heart-wrenching review.

Miriam was a very bright and accomplished woman in her twenties who approached me after the death of her father. She was anxious and confused over how to respond. He had been a terribly abusive parent, mostly verbally, putting down both her and her sister repeatedly. To the outside world, he was a charming, engaging, successful businessman, but to Miriam and her sister, he was an ogre, a volcano of anger, exploding unpredictably for unclear reasons. He told his two daughters how ugly and stupid they were, how much money they cost him, what a bitch their mother was (they were divorced), and ironically enough, how ungrateful they were despite all he had done for them, and especially how terrible they were when they distanced themselves from him as they entered their college years. And now that putrid Papa was dead, what exactly did they, Miriam and her sister, owe him? Now that he was gone, must they go to the funeral, sit shivah, recite kaddish for eleven months? For Miriam, religious tradition served as a secure footing in an otherwise unreliable world, and yet the extent to which the tradition would have her honor a parent, under the circumstances, was suddenly no longer apparent. In the end, she did not attend the funeral or the burial, but she did recite kaddish for the year, mourning a relationship that had died long ago. Did she fulfill the mitzvah of honoring her father or not? What would a revealed law demand of her?

Perhaps God did answer Miriam in her struggle to do what is right. The response did not happen in a single moment. It took a long time, several meetings, lengthy discussions, and a lot of tears. The discussion would not have sounded like anything too familiar in the yeshiva, the world where pairs of students argue the meaning of Torah. There were no rapid-fire quotations in Aramaic nor any consulting multiple commentators on passages from the Bible. But the passionate discussions I had with Miriam were no less than those of the boys in the yeshiva, and the substance of the debate was no less sacred. What's more, this was no academic discussion. This was verbal sparring that would ultimately impact on how this woman would feel for years following the death of that abusive man. In the end, Miriam, who could have easily slammed the study door in my face and walk out angry and resentful, found a way to use traditional forms to mourn the death of a relationship that now could never be restored. It was her way of honoring her father. And thus God's will was revealed. Or discovered. Or both.

The notion that the sacred may be discovered within the secular is not an accepted doctrine within liberal Jewish circles. The Jewish community, in general, still sees a distinction between the two realms and as such, does not allow the one to impinge on the other. The result of this rigid barrier between the sacred and secular has not served the interests of either. The sacred is dismissed as ignorance or superstition. The secular kills reverence and awe, sacrificing mystery on the altar of scientific explanation. In the end, both domains suffer. Moreover, how can the two ever be reconciled if the one emanates from Revelation, God's willing self-disclosure to humanity, and the other from empiricism, or the discovery of truths which are seemingly there but not yet exposed?

For a person with a contemporary faith, revelation and discovery need not be two distinct domains: Discovery is Revelation. It's not either/or. Rather, the one leads to the other. When we discover a truth, we have exposed another one of God's prophets, as *Berikh Shemei* assures us. Torah is Truth and Truth is Torah.

The time is long overdue for us to recite a blessing before studying any of the so-called secular disciplines, in the same way a blessing would be recited before studying Torah. We could use the same blessing as has been in vogue for centuries. But in recognition of our having expanded the idea of Torah to realms never before included in the definition, we need not be too particular in imitating a blessing that already exists. We can create something new, perhaps something like this:

Thank You, God, for allowing me the opportunity granted my ancestors, to see the extraordinary in the ordinary, the miracle in the material, and Your Revelation in human Discoveries. May those around me be so blessed as I myself am blessed. And may this Revelation of You lead to a world at peace.

The academic purists will undoubtedly bristle at the thought of ascribing God to anything having to do with science. And when demands are made for further clarification, it will be challenging. How do we actually explain the connection between God and galaxies, the Maker of Heaven and Earth with the molecules of earth and heaven, or the God of Faithfulness with Heisenberg's Uncertainty Principle? We can't explain it because there is no explanation. It's never been explainable. It's all a matter of faith. But the connection is there. And know that in every Discovery, God is Revealed.

• • • • •

TO THE REVELATION SKEPTIC

Science does not replace Revelation. It is an aspect
of Revelation.
Where truth is discovered, God is revealed.

5 THE MESSIAH SKEPTIC

There's no such thing as a messiah.

Among the most common prayers recited, are prayers for healing. Prayers are recited for those who are ill, family and friends, and more often than not, people pray for their own recovery, particularly when faced with surgery or serious illness. Though people recite these prayers on their own, many call clergy to do it for them, as if a prayer from a clergyperson will in some way be more effective than one recited in their own hearts. I get these calls on a weekly basis and happily recite these prayers known as *mi shebeirakh* prayers. *Mi shebeirakh* simply means "The One who blessed" and constitutes the first two words of the conventional prayer for healing. It essentially calls on the One who blessed our ancestors to bless also...and here would be inserted the name of the one who is ill.

When the question is raised about the effectiveness of these prayers, I invariably affirm their efficacy on all sorts of levels. A *Mi Shebeirakh* recited means that there is someone in the community who cares about an ailing individual, that there is a community that cares about that person, that the patient who knows that such prayers are being recited is in some way fortified by that knowledge, and I would go so far as to claim that the positive energy created by such prayers sticks with those who have recited it, such that it is carried from one place to another. When the prayer is carried into the confines of the sick room, the energy can only help.

"Rabbi, you have to say a *mi shebeirakh* for my mother, because I know your *mi shebeirakh* prayers work." This woman, ashen with anxiety and deeply solicitous of my services, could not remove her sorrowful gaze from me until she received my assent. Of course, there was no doubt that I would accommodate her. I wanted to first settle her own agitation as well as create that good energy for her mother, but I felt disingenuous in confirming the request without comment. "Ellen, of course I will say a prayer for Mom. I will say a few. But remember they are not 'my *mi shebeirakh* prayers.' I recite the words, but the healing comes from God."

"Rabbi, I know your *mi shebeirakh* prayers work. They always do. Thank you, thank you," and so the conversation ended.

Over the years, I have noticed a tendency by many to grant far greater power to certain people than they actually deserve. It's not necessarily a Jewish phenomenon as much as it is a human phenomenon, and one sees it in all aspects of life. It is the tendency to idolize the athlete, the talented trader, the charismatic politician, the insightful academic, and even a clergyperson. These are the people who in the minds of "ordi-nary mortals" will make that impossible touchdown, net thou-sands of dollars in a single day, marshal the disheveled forces of Washington, D.C., crystallize an historical development into some pristine and compelling precis, and grab the attention of the heavenly hosts for the purpose of healing the sick and ailing. This sort of hero-worship is deeply troubling because it just isn't true. Sure, we all have our individual talents, and God knows that some have received what would appear to be an extra helping, but the bottom line is that no one is that talented all the time and from a Jewish perspective, no one is any more naturally connected to God than anyone else.

It was Joseph of Egyptian fame who clearly made this point in his nascent political career. Having been identified as the only person in all of Egypt who really knew how to inter-pret dreams, he was hauled out of a two-year imprisonment and brought before Pharaoh to interpret the latter's troubling dreams of blighted sheaves and dying cows. "And Pharaoh said to Joseph, 'I have had a dream, and there is no one who can interpret it. But I have heard it said of you that for you to hear a dream is to tell its meaning.' Joseph answered Pharaoh, 'Not I! God will see to Pharaoh's welfare.'"[16] Joseph's words were a sign that he had matured from his initial character as the younger tattle-telling favored brother into a more mature and chastened persona. More importantly, he attributed his talents not to himself but to God, a sure sign of his newfound humility

---

16   Genesis 41:15-16

and a testament to the spiritual truth he clearly owned, that we should never be taken for greater than we really are.

The human tendency to idolize is complemented by the desire of others to be idolized. There is no underestimating the temptation of vanity, arrogance, and hubris to which humans are especially drawn. The idolizers and the idolized are bound in a rather enervating dynamic in which both cheapen their humanity by the one exploiting the other. In those cases, it is eminently satisfying to watch the veil of the arrogant ripped away when circumstances conspire to allow it. This is essentially the scene from "The Wizard of Oz" when Toto, Dorothy's terrier, clamps down on a curtain that reveals the man operating the great Oz. "Pay no attention to that man behind the curtain!" says the man behind the curtain, the man who has created this illusion of power and greatness. "Who are you?" Dorothy demands, forcing the truth from one who has grown far too comfortable with his own deceit. And as our intrepid heroes discover, the great Oz is only an "ordinary man," or as Scarecrow puts it a bit more dramatically, a "humbug."

All this is a prelude to an examination of another way people have fallen into the temptation of idolization: creating messiahs. The word "messiahs" is written deliberately and not in the singular for throughout history, in fact, a number of people have declared themselves so, and thousands of others have accepted the assertion and proselytized on behalf of their hero. This is a substantial aspect of religiosity in Judaism as well as in other faith traditions, so looking into the veracity of the messianic phenomenon is worthwhile, particularly because in modern times, it raises questions about the integrity of religion. Does religion teach great truths or does it give license to the humbugs of the world? What is at the root of the messianic impulse?

Legend has it that many years ago, a woman received a divine communication that she would give birth to a very special boy, the son of God, whose birth was accompanied by special supernatural signs. The boy impressed the religious authorities with his wisdom. He soon left home and became a circuit preacher, moving people to leave the material world behind for a more spiritual existence. The young man acquired followers who thought him divine, and he further gained a reputation by delivering charismatic sermons coupled with performing miracles like healing the sick, casting out demons, and raising the dead. As time passed, he suffered at the hand of enemies who brought him to the Roman authorities on a series of charges, which led to his death. And yet, following his death, he reappeared again as a living soul before ascending to heaven. This is a story that any Christian would recognize, but they would be mistaken to identify this miracle man as Jesus. It is the story of Apollonius of Tyana (15-100 CE), a pagan philosopher who worshiped the Greek gods. His followers knew about Jesus, though dismissed Jesus as a mere magician. They certainly did not accept the claim that Jesus was the son of God. That title, or some variation thereof, was reserved for Apollonius.

In the ancient world, stories about messiahs abound. It was not uncommon to think of certain people as figures of salvation, or for others to declare themselves as such. The idea of messiah is central to Christian belief and practice, but the whole idea of messiah is born of Jews and Jewish thought. The Christians, the clear majority of whom began as Jews, took the idea of messiah and elevated it to a central position in Christian thinking. Moreover, Christians determined that the messiah's arrival on earth established a new order in religious observance and belief. Some say that should the messiah ever appear in our lifetime, the first order of questions would begin with: Is this your first or a return visit? That will be one very interesting day, but history suggests that it won't happen in our lifetime. As the old joke goes, there was a little town in Russia that hired a man to stand at the city gate to wait for the messiah so the townspeople would be the first to know of his coming. The man was paid one ruble a month, a paltry sum at best. One day a friend of his approached and said, "Shloimie, one ruble a month? You could feed horses in a barn and be paid more! To which Shloimie replied, "I know, the pay is lousy, but the job security is fabulous."

What is a messiah? This, in and of itself, is no easy question to answer since one person's messiah is another person's pretender. Messiah is a word lifted from the Hebrew, *mashiah*, and it literally means "one who is anointed." Anointing is the act of taking some substance, like olive oil, and pouring it or smearing it on a person in order to distinguish that person in some specified way. Oil was the most common substance used in ancient times, though blood was also used, and in some cultures, milk or melted butter. The term "smear" is used deliberately, as anoint is a word borrowed from the French, itself borrowed from the Latin root *unguere*, meaning to smear. The English word "unctuous" comes from the same root and means either excessively pious or moralistic, or oily and greasy. In any event, the act of anointing was to take some specific substance and smear it on a priest or a king simply to distinguish the leader. It did not carry with it any pretension of divinity or cosmic greatness beyond marking a person as a religious or political leader. According to the Bible, one needn't even be Jewish to be so entitled. Cyrus, the king of Persia, is referred to as God's *mashiah* or "anointed one."[17] In this way, Isaiah grants Cyrus, a polytheistic secular leader, an esteemed stature within the Jewish community. But the term as used within the biblical period did not have the same connotations as it would today. As a matter of fact, in chapter 61, Isaiah refers to himself as having been anointed by God, thus in essence acknowledging that he himself was a messiah. And yet no Israelite at the time, and certainly no biblical scholar today, would refer to Isaiah as the messiah in the sense the term is typically understood by Christians.

Isaiah is an important prophet for anyone engaged in messianic studies. Many Christian scholars see in the chapters of Isaiah a portent to Jesus' ministry, particularly in an image

---

17   cf. Isaiah, chapter 45:1

that Isaiah cultivates known as the Suffering Servant. Chapter 53 speaks of a man who was wounded because of humanity's sins, whose grave was set among the wicked, and whose mental and spiritual fortitude was such that he would not complain in spite of the torture inflicted upon him. This suffering servant made himself a guilt offering to God, bore the punishment of all people and thus cleansed human beings of their sins. It sounds very Christological and more or less fits the synoptic gospels' tales of Jesus. But the story, written some 500 years before Jesus, was written in the past tense, making it difficult to frame it as a prophecy for a coming messiah. Jews typically understood the Suffering Servant not as a forecast, but as a symbol of Israel and all the trials it had endured. More specifically, they understood the Suffering Servant as the suffering Israelites of the Northern Kingdom of Israel, also known by its capital city, Samaria, who lost their country and their autonomy by an Assyrian rout (722 BCE). Through military defeat and subsequent exile, the Israelites suffered a great deal. And somehow the prophet managed to see in all that a message of hope and he delivers that message to Israel.

Isaiah's message is deeply comforting, and it rings with a universal tonality. Most people are willing to endure hardship if their pain and suffering is in some way purposeful; that is, it will lead to something greater and better than that which they are now experiencing. In modern terms, parents might be willing to work two or even three jobs if they can earn enough to send their kids to college, and such a goal is of central importance to them. Soldiers might risk their lives in war if it will secure the safety of their nation. Cancer patients will undergo all the miserable side effects of chemo if it will cleanse them of this disease and grant them more years to live and enjoy life. People will tolerate suffering if the suffering is meaningful. And that is the thrust of Isaiah's message. He is essentially turning to his audience and saying, "You were driven from your land. You lost your jobs. You have been subjected to an unsympathetic empire, but not to worry. God accepts your suffering as a collective sin-offering that cleanses you of your sins and sets you aright with the Lord. Do not despair—your suffering has a deeper meaning." That's the Jewish understanding of the narrative. Later Christian scholars will read into it an entirely different narrative, understanding within the imagery a harbinger of the coming of the Christ. The way so many people have interpreted and reinterpreted these ancient texts is what has made the biblical narrative so rich and magical in its own right.

Nonetheless, from a Jewish perspective alone, there is no clear and unequivocal reference in the Prophets to a messiah, as Christians would understand that term. Yet the early Christians were Jews who were intimately involved in the reinterpretation of these texts. Two factors came into play which led Jews to an idea of a messiah who is a glorious, divine figure of redemption and salvation. The first is that the Judeans living under Roman rule hoped for a new political order that would secure peace, assure prosperity, return exiles from abroad back to their homeland in Palestine, and restore the political autonomy they had lost centuries earlier. In other words, the people were not terribly happy with foreign kings—at the time of Jesus, Roman emperors—who imposed taxes, enforced conscription, confiscated property at will, compromised the purity of the Temple's environs, and both minimized and marginalized the involvement of local Jews in their own political destiny. Empires were remarkably vulnerable to corruption and political bungling as are so many monarchies or totalitarian regimes. But 2000 years ago, a democratically elected government which was a tad more accountable than its non-democratic forebears was not an option. The best government one could hope for was one run by a just and fair king--a generous king, a compassionate king, perhaps one who would tax reasonably and not enslave men for purposes of war or building projects. Beyond that, what would a good king look like? This is where the second factor kicks in. The good king would generate all the utopian characteristics of a prophetic vision that once again placed the Jewish people on top of the world. The king, this messiah, would usher in an age in which everyone believed in the one God, and he would render the Jewish people the central authority for all spiritual guidance, and maybe this king would even banish death. And this dream did not begin with disappointment in Roman rule. In spite of periods of calm and peace, the Jews were not too enamored with Greek rule (second century BCE), were not in love with the Hasmoneans who succeeded them, and they definitely had their issues with Rome. The dream of a good king who would save the people and redeem them from oppression and hardship was a sustaining fantasy. Despite difficult times, the messiah was just beyond the city gate. And it was not only the Jews who prayed for this messiah. There were many people who hoped for that one magic man to come and save humanity from itself and as such, messianic themed legends proliferated. Apollonius of Tyana was one such legend.

When Jesus is referred to as Christ, he is conferred with a Greek title meaning *mashiah* or "the anointed one." This is the definition of the Greek term *khristos*: "the anointed one." Christians are the people who believe in the Christ, that is, the messiah, and in their case, a very specific messiah. Although the New Testament does not treat the Jews with great kindness, the fact is that the initial Christians were almost all Jewish. The twelve apostles were all Jews. The divide between the Christians and Jews came about due to a disagreement over what it takes to become a Christian. The earliest Christians had no doubt that the only way to be a Christian was to first be a Jew—which for gentiles meant conversion, or more specifically, circumcision, immersion in a *mikveh* or ritual pool, and a commitment to follow *Halakhah* or Jewish law. But there were other Jews, the disciple Paul the prime example, who said that because Jesus needed to be Christ for everybody, not just the Jews, the barriers of entry into the covenant had to be lowered. According to Paul, simply by putting one's faith in Jesus as the Christ would gain one's entry into the community of Christians and obviate the need for circumcision or following the law. One might choose conversion and adherence to the law, but it needn't serve as a barrier to joining the Christian fold. Paul's views prevailed, and as non-Jews increasingly identified as Christians, Jews increasingly did not, and that was the beginning of a divide that would evolve into centuries of hatred, oppression, and contempt.

To be sure, it's not as if the Jewish community was of one mind on the issue of Jesus. Some were believers and some were not. In his time, Jesus was controversial, challenging the authority and integrity of the priests. And if he was the messiah, where was that era of universal peace and prosperity, of the return of the people of Israel to their homeland, of *tehiyat hameitim,* the resurrection of the dead? What kind of underachiever was this messiah? Would there ever be a messiah that could live up to the messianic hype? Jews had their doubts. It is no wonder that Rabbi Yohanan ben Zakkai (1st century CE), who is most credited for saving Judaism after the destruction of the Temple, instructed the community that given the choice between planting a tree or running to greet the messiah, plant the tree first.[18] Rabbi Yohanan ben Zakkai's priorities reveal something about the rather jaded Jewish view toward messiahs.

In Turkey today, there is a small group of Muslims who secretly observe a form of Judaism known as Sabbateanism. Sabbateanism is based on the teachings and legends of Shabbetai Tzvi, the 17th century Ottoman Jew who claimed to

---

18   Avot d' Rabbi Natan B31

be the messiah, and who actually amassed a substantial following until he decided to convert to Islam. His conversion disrupted an otherwise faithful following and threw many of his adherents into spiritual turmoil.

There have been no lack of claimants to messiahship over the centuries. There was Shimon Bar Kochba in the second century, Moses of Crete in the fifth century, Serene of Syria in the eighth century, David Alroy of the 12th century, Abraham Abulafia of the 13th century, Jacob Frank of the 18th century, and the only woman claiming to be the Jewish messiah, Jacob Frank's daughter, Eve Frank, an alleged 19th century Jewish messiah. In modern times, there are those who believe that the seventh Lubavitcher rebbe, Rabbi Menachem Mendel Schneerson (1902-1994) is the messiah and will someday return. This again points to the deep faith some hold in finding or identifying that one individual who will act as the savior for themselves personally and for the world at large. How Schneerson messianism will end, if it ever will, is a chapter yet to be written. As for the majority of previous messianic movements, they ended either in communal disappointment at best or in a variety of disasters, Jews being punished or so divided among themselves as to cause communal disruption that took years to heal.

Moses Maimonides' idea of the messiah was a fairly stripped-down, unimpressive character. Maimonides writes: "One should not presume that the messianic king must work signs and wonders, bring about new phenomena in the world, resurrect the dead, or perform other similar deeds. That's not how it will be."[19] What, then, would a messiah do? According to Maimonides:

> In the future, the Messianic king will arise and restore the Davidic dynasty to its original sovereignty. He will build the Temple and gather the exiles of Israel. During his tenure, the statutes of old will again be in force. We will offer sacrifices, and observe the Sabbatical and Jubilee years in all their particulars as outlined in the Torah.[20]

Presumably, a modest messiah is better than no messiah, and Jews were very much taken by the twelfth principle of Maimonides' thirteen principles of faith, composed in the 13th century, which affirmed faith in this elusive, forever coming messiah.

Six centuries later, there were a few Jews who had grown weary of waiting for this tarrying messiah. Zionism might be referred to as the un-messianic movement, a movement that basically eschewed faith in a messiah that would restore Jews to their ancient homeland. After 1900 years of disappointment and failed messiahs, it was time for Jews to return to Israel of their own accord. Jews would take charge of their own fate, begin the return to Israel sans the assistance of any messianic figure, and thereby create a new age free of anti-Semitism.

---

19   Mishneh Torah, Hilkhot Melakhim 11:3
20   Mishneh Torah, Hilkhot Melakhim 11:1

Given the tradition, this was religious heresy. The Zionists' denial of a messiah initially earned them the contempt of religious Jews the world over, a view which softened over the years as their methods not only bore success but began to concretize the very aspirations of religious Jews for centuries—a return to a Jewish homeland and the rebirth of an authentically Jewish culture. The Zionists, empowered by the Haskalah (the Jewish Enlightenment) and a secularism that freed them from strict adherence to religious doctrine, did more to restore Jewish autonomy in a single century than a multitude of fervent prayers for the messiah did in 1900 years. Zionists had no use for a messiah who tarried for centuries. While Zionism was successful in establishing a Jewish state, one of its fundamental objectives, a world free of anti-Semitism, is a dream yet to be realized.

The Zionist rejection of the messiah may have been a harbinger of a revolution in religious idealism because most socially active liberal Jews do not believe in a messiah. They no longer think of the messiah as a person who will usher in an age of peace or prosperity, an age of understanding or mutual respect. But for those who do think about the messiah, the belief has evolved into *yemei hamashiah,* a messianic period, a period which would be very much akin to everything the *mashiah* would have materialized, but by means of an agency other than a single man or woman. This messianic period would begin when people work together for justice and peace, and cooperate with each other toward the common good of all.

There would be no messiah per se, but there would be many working with a messianic fervor and intention.

There is a danger in promoting *yemei hamashiah* too eagerly, deluding oneself into thinking the age of universal peace and happiness is just floating on the horizon, soon to dock in the home port. The whole idea smacks of '60's utopianism, albeit sans the free sex and rampant usage of hallucinogens (though both may have contributed to the delusion of world peace in the first place). But there is a truth in this adage: if you can think it, then you can believe it. If you believe it, you can talk about it. And if you talk about it, you can possibly create it. And that is a matter of faith. *Yemei hamashiah* consecrates the challenge to act in a messianic vein without the delusion of actually claiming oneself to be a messiah.

The fact is that the great men and women of the day ultimately disappoint. Their flawed humanity will be exposed. History proves over and over again one simple, heretical, fact— there are no messiahs. The way in which great people tend to fall short, the way icons are smashed, and powerful ones tumble from grace remind us not to place one's salvation in the hands of any one person. The Bible also knew this to be true when it observed: "Put not your trust in princes, or mortal man who cannot save. His breath departs, he dissolves into dust, and on that day his plans turn to nothing."[21]

There are movements of people who decide that the time has come to change, to improve, to repair, to grow, to evolve.

---

21 Psalm 146:3-4

Sometimes these movements do what they intend to do and sometimes they do just the opposite. Human evolution itself is a messy business; it does not move in a linear fashion but zig-zags and detours and follows anything but the shortest distance between two points. It is the godly spark within us that ultimately moves us, with the passage of time, to more sophisticated and deeper levels of living and human interaction.

The claim that there is no messiah should not be understood as a generalized criticism of those whose faith rests on a belief in a messiah. To the extent that this belief moves them to acts of kindness and charity, then it is certainly a belief worthy of a sacred stature. This is how we ought to think of the faith to which our Christian neighbors and friends adhere. But it's important to remember that Jewish tradition energizes in the same direction albeit via an alternative fuel, and that is the energy created by a direct relationship with God, free of intermediaries. This idea, much more so than the messianic ideal, has its roots in the prophets as well. As the prophet Jeremiah declares:

> But this is the covenant that I will make with the House of Israel after those days—declares the Lord: I will put My Teaching into their inmost being and write it upon their hearts. Then I will be their God, and they shall be My people. No longer will they need to teach one another and say to one

another, "Know the Lord"; for all of them, from the least of them to the greatest, shall know Me— declares the Lord.[22]

This beautiful, powerful passage doesn't refer to any kind of messiah, yet points to a messianic era, a time when there will be no need to consult some holy person as to how to act. The right path, the good path, the righteous path will surface almost intuitively. That is a vision of *yemei hamashiah* which moderns can embrace. It idolizes no one, and in truth, does not even idolize a community. It requires no grand illusion that success is in any one person's hands, for chances are that is a supreme fairy tale, unworthy of a tradition that promotes truth. But it does not abandon hope in a world that can improve if only people would agree that the only messianic movement worth promoting is the one that encourages ordinary people to pursue extraordinary objectives in the attempt to make the kind of world that some envision a messiah was born to create.

• • • • •

TO THE MESSIAH SKEPTIC

There is no personal messiah; there never was one, and there never will be. Whether we believe in the messiah as a person or a period, we can all agree to strive for peace and justice, for a world worthy of the messiah.

---

22   Jeremiah 31:33-34

6 THE CHOSENNESS SKEPTIC

*Please don't refer to us as the Chosen
People. It makes us appear arrogant or
superior, or both, and it's not right in an age
of tolerance and mutual respect.*

Since 1996, Jeremy Cowan has been producing a certified
kosher brand of beer under the name He'brew, which today is
produced by the Shmaltz Brewing Company, located in Clifton
Park, New York. I was amused by one of their commercials
which advertised themselves as "He'brew—the Chosen Beer."
Of course, this is a playful twist on a time-honored or time-cen-
sured tag line of the Jewish people: "the Chosen People."

The ancient concept of chosenness has its roots firmly
planted in the Torah. As Moses says to the Children of Israel,
"For you are a people holy to the Lord your God: the Lord your
God chose you from all other peoples on the face of the earth
to be His treasured people."[23] There's nothing like being picked
to serve on the team for feeling good about oneself. And in this
case, there's no one better than God to act as team captain.

---

23   Deuteronomy 14:2

God, after all, would be the ultimate Chooser. To be chosen on God's team conveys an honor like no other, and the Jewish people have known this for generations. On the other hand, insofar as people have either construed or misconstrued the idea to their own liking, chosenness has not always redounded to the Jewish people's benefit. As the character Tevye in the film "Fiddler on the Roof" says, "I know. We are Your chosen people. But, once in a while, can't You choose someone else?"

Tevye had a point. In his own simple way of looking at a complex world that was rapidly changing before him, he understood implicitly that chosenness was an attribute of Jews and their peculiar self-conception. In fact, a good case could be made that Jews believe in a God who does look to others and who establishes relationships with others, for ultimately, the "Jewish God" is not the God of the Jewish people alone, but the God of all people. This idea also has its roots in the biblical literature. God has a relationship with the non-Jewish wizard Balaam, hired to curse the Jewish people but blesses them instead. God has a relationship with Job who is not portrayed as a Jew, but as a righteous person whom God respects. And God has a relationship with all the sinning Ninevites, sparing them from punishment, and this after God's Jewish prophet, Jonah, had warned them of imminent punishment. The best way to read all these instances of God's relationships with others is as a form of chosenness, but as a chosenness of a different character. One might put it this way: God potentially chooses everyone, but for different purposes. Jewish chosenness is therefore in some way unique to the Jewish people, but having been chosen is not unique to the Jews.

One Shabbat, my former congregation in Montclair, NJ, had the honor of hosting Sister Rose Thering (1920-2006), a Roman Catholic nun who had earned for herself a stellar reputation for her Catholic-Jewish interfaith work and her bold teaching about and speaking against anti-Semitism. She was a professor at Seton Hall University and an energetic, charismatic soul. One of the synagogue's members approached me during services and asked if I would give Sister Rose an *aliyah* (i.e., an honor to recite a blessing) to the Torah. I promptly said I would not, surprised that anyone would even think it proper to do so. He demanded an explanation. I explained that the very essence of receiving such an honor involved the recitation of a blessing which describes the honoree as having been "chosen among all the peoples" via the instrument of Torah. The member countered, "But God gave the Torah to all people and certainly Sister Rose believes in that Torah as well." I couldn't disagree with that but as I explained, the "chosenness" of the Torah blessing refers to a specific way of life, a way of looking at the world, and Sister Rose was not a part of that chosenness, even though there was no question that God had a purpose for her and that she was doing God's work on earth. The member knew I wasn't budging on this matter of ritual, granting a nun an *aliyah* to the Torah, but did end the conversation by looking out at the congregation, about sixty-five good people one and all, and concluded by saying, "I dunno, Rabbi, Sister Rose loves the Jews more than anyone else in this sanctuary."

The principle of chosenness makes many Jews uncomfortable, even embarrassed. It's as if feeling special were a zero-sum game—as one group feels more special, another group must feel less. In a world of mutual respect, something we all aspire to, no group should feel superior to another. But must chosenness be construed as the distinction of superiority? The meaning of chosenness depends a great deal on what an individual makes of it. Jews have a reputation for having excelled through the years, sometimes under the most adverse of conditions, and whether this is due to divine blessing, natural talent, or the work of some covert publicity firm is up for debate. But one could look at such successes and explain it all as the result of chosenness, as if Jews had no other fate in life but to succeed. Perhaps the chosenness of the Jewish people has led them to successes and achievements others have found unattainable, but this conclusion could only be drawn by ignoring the many failures, shortcomings, and sorrows that have beset the people over the years. If chosenness is understood as conferring inevitable success, then blood libels, expulsions, pogroms, and the murder of 6,000,000 Jews during the period of the Shoah, the Holocaust, ought to throw a bucket's worth of freezing water on such a definition.

To truly appreciate chosenness, the whole idea of what it means to be chosen by God must be explored. From a critical and contemporary perspective, there is good reason to doubt that God ever pointed to the Jewish people and said, "You're My chosen ones!" It's an image vulnerable to the most egregious parodies as captured in the following doggerel of disputed authorship:

> How odd
>
> Of God
>
> To choose
>
> The Jews

An edgy rejoinder, sometimes attributed to Leo Rosten (1908-1997), the American writer and humorist, sought to explain the oddity:

> It's not
>
> So odd,
>
> The Goyim
>
> Annoy'im

Rosten, whether intentionally or inadvertently, hit upon the very irritant that generations of non-Jews were none too pleased about, this idea that God had some special and unique relationship with the Jews, placing everyone else in position number two, at best. And this sense of disappointment, like the underdog in a sibling rivalry, generated a host of questions along the order of: What makes the Jews so special? Why would God play favorites? But umbrage of this nature assumes that the act of chosenness was history. It's a fantasy conception of a God in the heavens above, pointing downward to the Jews below, and proclaiming the Jews "the Chosen Ones." Our rational selves are going to resist framing such mythology, albeit dramatic and moving, as fact. Resorting to a critical and demythologized understanding of chosenness would demand a reverse scenario. It would conceive of the Jewish people on the earth below pointing heavenward, making some conscious choice to connect with God, but fashioning it as a choice that God, not the people, made. And thus the more common rejoinder to God's surprising choices:

> It's not
>
> So odd,
>
> The Jews
>
> Chose God

Given this conception, a dynamic in which the direction of choosing is not from heaven downward but from earth heavenward, we can begin to explore the true nature of chosenness. Chosenness is what could rightfully be described as the Jewish people's foundational myth.

Foundational myths are those myths which help explain why a particular entity has come to be, like a city or a state, and what attributes characterize that particular entity. Any number of ancient foundational myths connected cities with gods. The goddess Athena, for example, is deeply connected with ancient Athens. At a time when the city was without divine protection, two gods vied for the honor—Athena and the god Poseidon, god of the sea. The two were passionate about securing the right to guard the city and were on the verge of battle until Athena, known also as the goddess of wisdom, proposed a non-violent contest. Each god would present a gift to the city, and whichever gift was favored by the citizens, that god would win rights to rule and protect the city. Poseidon, with lots of water at his disposal, brought the city hot steam, which was useful in many ways. Athena, in contrast, planted an olive seed, which would eventually produce a multitude of olive trees, a tremendous source of income for the city. Athena's gift was deemed the superior gift and thus she became the patron goddess of the city, and the city was named in her honor. This myth recognizes the Athenians as people who would choose to resolve conflict peacefully and who view olives and their by-products as a godly gift.

Rome, too, has a foundational myth that the city began with a miraculous story of twins, Romulus and Remus, whose father was Mars, the god of war. The two were doomed to be drowned in the Tiber River, but the trough into which they were set floated down river and the two were discovered and raised by a she-wolf and a woodpecker who sustained them. They grew up to be two tough kids, took actions that addressed the injustice they and their families had been dealt, and then eventually founded a city that would become Rome. And so here is a myth that points to the essence of what it means to be Roman—ready for war, prepared to redress injustice, and ultimately connected to something divine. Such a myth may just make any would-be attackers think twice about an offensive strike.

It doesn't matter if citizens of a particular city or state are mindful of the foundational myth because the whole rhythm and values of a culture will have already been shaped by the myths themselves. Some might argue that the values and rhythms of a particular entity will give rise to a particular kind of myth. This is almost a "Which came first, the chicken or the egg?" debate, but it does show the interdependence of social values with the myths of a specific culture. The two are interdependent. It's not unlike the foundational myth of George Washington admitting to chopping down the cherry tree, which explains the American emphasis on honesty. But was it the myth that established American honesty or American honesty that gave rise to the myth? The question is best pondered than answered, and suffice to say that until this day, coverups in America are almost always viewed worse than the crime itself. Committing a crime is bad. Lying about committing the crime is worse. That's what George taught Americans: those who tell the truth typically come out ahead. Or, perhaps, that's the message that has been inserted into America's first president's apocryphal youth.

Chosenness is one of the Jewish people's foundational myths. In fact, Jews have several foundational stories, usually expressed as covenants between God and Abraham, or Jacob, or Moses, or the entire Israelite people. In each case the covenant or *brit,* a holy contract, bound the Jewish people to God and vice versa. Covenant is a two-way agreement, God being godly to the people in exchange for their moral and spiritual allegiance. The covenant is almost always construed as initiated by God, with God choosing an individual or nation, and their descendants. Covenants actually make chosenness less a reward and more an obligation. The covenant makes no guarantee of unconditional love. To the contrary, chosenness is a very conditional love. That is why the prophet Amos quotes God in a stern reprimand of the people of Israel as follows: "You alone have I singled out of all the families of the earth—that is why I will call you to account for all your iniquities."[24] This is chosenness, but a chosenness that demands accountability for all one's moral failings.

During college, I was sitting in the kitchen of my rabbi's home with a few friends, discussing the wearing of a *kippah* in public. At the time, a number of my peers were experimenting with wearing a *kippah* outside the safety of the synagogue. This was a big deal. Wearing a *kippah* in private, at home or at the synagogue, was gutless. But to don a *kippah* and walk around a lake or stroll down the mall of the university campus, that was a whole other level of observance and identity. Confessing to my true feelings about the matter, I chimed in with my own take on the issue: "Wearing a *kippah* in public, in class, at the ball park? I'd feel as if I would have to be on my best behavior all the time!" to which a very wise and loving Shirley Abelson, my rabbi's wife, responded, "What's wrong with that?!" Four words: what's, wrong, with, that. What a fabulous retort to my anxieties about behaving, and what a brilliant summary of chosenness—having to behave in only the best manner possible, all the time!

------

24   Amos 3:2

I often find myself sitting with a bar or bat mitzvah family, helping them through the challenge of assigning honors to relatives with as little political collateral damage as possible. During one such episode, the mother of the bat mitzvah asked about honoring her brother with an *aliyah* to the Torah. I told her that would be fine—why would she even ask? She explained further that he had a very close relationship with his niece, the bat mitzvah, but that a number of years ago, he converted to Christianity. That certainly explained why the question was raised. At that point I told her that we would have to find another way to honor Uncle Bobby, but that an honor to the Torah would be out of the question. The mother of the bat mitzvah was relatively familiar with Jewish law and questioned me further on the predicament. She acknowledged the family's and her own disappointment with Uncle Bobby's conversion, but then raised the Jewish principle that even though Jews may sin, they nonetheless remain Jews. She had a point and supported it with a bona fide Jewish principle—once you are a Jew, it's hard, almost impossible, to leave the fold. I could tell that she really wanted her brother to have an *aliyah,* but I wasn't sure if the objective was to honor him or reassure a family in pain that their Christian son, brother, uncle, etc. was still a member of the tribe. I told the mother, as diplomatically as I could, that her brother did remain a Jew, but in an age where we honor an individual's decisions about their personal identity, we cannot ignore his having made a conscious choice out of Judaism. Today, he has self-defined as a Christian. He has willingly and knowingly stepped away from Jewish chosenness into another realm of relationship with God. If we honor Uncle Bobby, it was going to be in some way other than his being called to the Torah, a rite that includes a blessing that emphasizes the giving of the Torah to the Jewish people as the ultimate act of chosenness.

The full first Torah blessing (there are two, one before and one following the reading of a Torah passage) reads: "Praised are You, Lord our God, Ruler of the universe, who has chosen us from among all peoples by giving us His Torah. Praised are You, Lord who gives the Torah." Mordecai Kaplan (1881-1983), co-founder of Reconstructionist Judaism and a long-time teacher of Torah at the Jewish Theological Seminary, altered the Torah blessings by removing any reference to chosenness. In the 1953 Reconstructionist edition of the prayer book, the Torah blessing reads: "Blessed be Thou, O Lord our God, King of the universe, who has brought us nigh to Thy service and hast given us Thy Torah. Blessed be Thou, O Lord, giver of the Torah." Absent is any reference to God having "chosen us from among all peoples." If there ever was a serious attempt to let both the Jewish and non-Jewish world know that chosenness was no longer integral to the Jewish ethos, it was Kaplan's decision to excise any reference to it from the Torah blessing. Dr. Kaplan's influence on contemporary Jewish life is beyond question, but his liturgical innovation would have little impact on those who would demonize Jews for their arrogance and superiority complex.

Within the field of Hate Studies, for which there is no appropriate Greek name though it deserves one, anti-Semitism must be among the most complex and fascinating forms of hatred. Michael Curtis, Rutgers University Distinguished Professor Emeritus of Political Science, observes:

> The uniqueness of anti-Semitism is that no other group of people in the world has been charged simultaneously with alienation from society and with cosmopolitanism, with being capitalist exploiters and agents of international finance and also revolutionary agitators, with having a materialist mentality and with being people of the Book, with acting as militant aggressors and with being cowardly pacifists uttering (in Michelet's phrase) "the groan of the slave," with adherence to a superstitious religion and with being agents of modernism, with upholding a rigid law and also being morally decadent, with being a chosen people and also having an inferior human nature, with both arrogance and timidity, with both individualism and communal adherence, with being guilty of the crucifixion of Christ and at the same time held to account for the invention of Christianity—as Nietzsche put it, "the ultimate Jewish consequence."[25]

---

25   Michael Curtis, "Introduction—Antisemitism: The Baffling Obsession," in *Antisemitism in the Contemporary World*, ed. Michael Curtis (Westview Press / Boulder and London), p. 4.

Most forms of hatred are at their base, irrational, but anti-Semitism is irrationality on an amphetamine rush. It is so preposterous that it would be humorous if we didn't know historically how deadly it can be. In spite of it all, Jews have survived and thrived. Some people have viewed the survival of the Jewish people as proof of their chosenness. Blaise Pascal (1623-1662), the French mathematician, physicist, and Catholic theologian, observed that in spite of the many powerful forces that have assaulted the Jews over the centuries, they persist, and thrive, and have outlived the greatest of civilizations from Greece to Rome.[26] The indestructibility of the Jewish people is observed by the prophet Jeremiah as follows: "Thus said the Lord, 'Who established the sun for light by day? The laws of moon and stars for light by night? Who stirs up the sea into roaring waves? The Lord of Hosts is His name. If these laws should ever be annulled by Me'—declares the Lord—'only then would the descendants of Israel cease to be a nation before Me for all time."[27] Jeremiah's writing stretches back some 2600 years and even at that time, he noted that there was something very unique about the Jewish people. They persist no matter the adversity. They persevere no matter the challenge. Nonetheless, it seems odd that the so-called blessing of chosenness could be understood as no more than survival. Survival to what end? What purpose? Bacteria, among the earliest life

---

26   Pascal, *Pensees*, translation by A.J. Krailsheimer, Penquin, Harmondsworth, 1968, p. 176-77.

27   Jeremiah 31:35-36

forms on earth, have also survived, and for much longer than the Jewish people.

To live the chosen life is to be mindful of just about everything you do and to do it in concert with what you believe God ultimately wants of you. It's not about "I'm better than you," the arrogance of such a position already a betrayal of chosenness, but it's about taking the very best ethical and spiritual paths available to us when confronted with a multiplicity of choices. That is a noble way to live and it is what chosenness has most directly meant for thinking, sensitive Jews. When Mordecai Kaplan expunged from the liturgy the common foundational myth of chosenness, he weakened the bonds that draw Jews together the world over.

My father was a senior partner in The State Tailors, a custom tailor shop in Minneapolis in the 1950's through the early '70's. As my father would describe it, it was a shop that made suits for either very wealthy people or "cripples." The business was such that he worked on Saturdays, but once a month, he had a Saturday off and took me to synagogue. For as long as I sat next to him in synagogue during his working years, he refused just about every Torah honor offered him. When I questioned him about this, he said that he was unworthy of accepting a Torah *aliyah* because he was not *shomer Shabbat*, a Sabbath observer. He thought that accepting an honor in synagogue, given his Shabbat sins, would be hypocritical. He certainly understood the Torah blessing to be a blessing about chosenness, but he equally understood his working on the Sabbath as a choice to violate the chosenness principle. The fact that his violation was more coerced than elective (the other partners were averse to his religious inclinations) was for him irrelevant. Frankly, it was his refusal to take an *aliyah* which in my own mind made him more worthy than others who did. For him it was a matter of integrity. It was hard to believe that anyone would have actually viewed his taking an *aliyah* as an act of hypocrisy, but he was not worried about what others might think, he was concerned only about how to guard the principles he himself held dear. To be chosen was to follow a specific spiritual and ethical path, to do so without hypocrisy and without an appetite for public accolades.

For those who would attack chosenness as an errant expression of arrogance and superiority, and thus worthy of the trash bin, I offer the following thought experiment. A child comes to a parent and says, "I'm untalented and of average intelligence. Everyone is better than me. I am in no way special. I don't stand out in anyway." How should a parent respond to that? Would the parent be justified in saying, "That's right, honey. You have no talents and you are not special. I don't know if everyone else is better than you, but let's just say that you are unremarkable, and always will be." Anyone who thinks this is good parenting should have their children placed in foster care. The fact is that all people need to feel special in some way and should be made to feel special. And when that overwhelming sense of un-remarkability grips an individual with tenacity, refusing to let go, that's the person who will soon be in need of serious psychotherapy for many years. All individuals and all people deserve to feel special in some way, and there is nothing wrong with that. There is, however, something very wrong in the attempt to deny another their specialness, especially when the specialness is innocuous, and serves as a basis for living a wholesome, moral, and mindful life, as the foundational myth of chosenness ideally does.

In truth, most Americans should be far more tolerant of Jewish chosenness given their own connection with a doctrine known as American Exceptionalism. This is the idea that unlike most countries in the rest of the world, the founding fathers set up a governmental structure so unique that America could not help but excel over all others in almost every pursuit imaginable, whether academics, commerce, technology or economics. Alexis de Tocqueville (1805-1859), the French diplomat and sociologist, wrote about it in his work, *Democracy in America.* The ironic difference between exceptionalism and chosenness is that exceptionalism really does imply a kind of superiority in a way that chosenness does not.

Certainly, there have been Jews who have abused the myth of chosenness and twisted it into an idea that it was never meant to be. And there certainly are non-Jews who have done likewise. The latter engage in age-old anti-Semitism which not only renders them racist, but devoid of creativity to boot, given anti-Semitism's tired trope of Jewish clannishness, materialism, sexual deviance, etc. As for Jews who would reject chosenness altogether, who would minimize the human need to feel special, who would dismiss chosenness as a challenge to live fully and morally, who would do violence to a foundational myth that binds Jews together geographically and throughout time, and who would turn a blind eye to how playfully Jews have integrated this myth into their lives, only one thing can be said: these Jews are in desperate need of a couple of He'brews, the Chosen Beer. And they might do well to down them with the members of Congregation Sukkat Shalom in Juneau, Alaska, who refer to themselves as "the Frozen Chosen."

• • • • •

TO THE CHOSENNESS SKEPTIC

Jews sometimes repudiate chosenness, a foundational myth of the Jewish people, for its presumed implication of Jewish superiority. There is, however, no reason to assert that chosenness necessarily implies superiority at all. It is much more a call for accountability to God. Chosenness deputizes Jews to leave this world better than they found it, and that is the fundamental raison d'etre of Jewish peoplehood.

7 THE MIRACLES SKEPTIC

So God split the Red Sea and that's how the Jews were saved?
There has to be some other explanation...

Blessings are not normally thought of as humorous, but were one to qualify, the first of the morning blessings would be a prime candidate: "Praised are You, Adonai our God, who accompanies us in our journey through the universe, and who has given the rooster the understanding to distinguish between day and night." Roosters? Really? First thing in the morning? The term for rooster in the Hebrew is *sekhvi,* and the sentiment of the blessing follows Job 38:36, which is one verse in a lengthy oration by God on the extraordinary nature of nature itself, over which a mere human exercises virtually no control. And part of that natural phenomenon is the "intelligence" of otherwise unintelligent animals (like a rooster), an intelligence that, as the oration would insinuate, is God-given and not human-made.

The rabbis, who were sticklers for reciting blessings at the precise time that the blessing ought to be recited—not a minute too soon or too late—did note that this is the blessing recited upon hearing the cock crow,[28] though the blessing, having made its way into the daily prayer book, is recited these days almost invariably sans an "alarm cock." The Jewish people must have been historically far more amenable to mornings (we refer now to a pre-Starbucks era), for I know any number of people who would sooner shoot the rooster than say a blessing upon hearing its early dawn cock-a-doodle-doo. The present custom is therefore much more civilized as the blessing need not be recited first thing in the morning and requires no initial audible crowing for its recitation. But rooster or no rooster, the blessing remains among the first of the morning blessings, the sages having seen great wisdom in praising God for the natural order, and one of its most marvelous creatures, the rooster, and the intelligence it demonstrates daily, with the rising of the sun.

There are those who need more startling and dramatic evidence of God's presence in the world than the mere mechanics of the animal kingdom. And they get it through the advent of miracles. Miracles are generally understood not so much as natural phenomena as supernatural phenomena, events that defy human reason or understanding. Miracles show up at just the right time, not a minute too soon or too late. In a 2009 Pew Research study on Mormons, 80% were found to fully believe in miracles, compared with only 47% of the general American population. Eighty percent is a high figure, but 47% is no

28   Berakhot 60a

insignificant percentage, surprisingly high for a culture that prides itself in its scientific and technological underpinnings. Millions of Americans have made room for the miraculous in their lives and they are not ashamed to say so. Stories of miracles abound in the media, and they force otherwise rational people to question their steadfast adherence to the scientific versus the allure of the mysterious and the inexplicable, perhaps even the passion to confirm evidence of God in everyday life.

In the early afternoon of March 7, 2015, first responders came to the Spanish Fork River in Utah to examine an overturned vehicle. While at the scene, two responders confirmed hearing a voice calling, "help me." In reaching the car, the 25-year-old driver, Lynn Jennifer Groesbeck, was found dead, but her 18-month-old daughter was hanging upside down in her car seat, just above the frigid waters, and very much alive. KUTV CBS affiliate confirmed that two officers had heard some voice, but it could not have come from the mother who most likely died on impact, or the little girl. One of the police officers said considering the toddler was hanging in that position for some fourteen hours, her survival, coupled with the mysterious call for help, was a miracle.

On March 25, 2010, Kate Ogg of Australia gave birth to twins, a boy and a girl. The girl survived but the boy did not, having been born in distress, and remaining unresponsive to twenty minutes of concentrated resuscitation. Having failed to revive the baby, doctors placed the baby over the mother's heart, and together with her husband David, gave them time to bid the baby farewell. After about five minutes, the baby began to move and the movements became more deliberate with time. The doctors, however, understood the movements to be reflexive rather than intentional, and gave the parents a few more minutes to absorb the sad reality. The "sad reality" also included the baby opening its eyes prompting the parents to further question the declaration of death. When the doctor finally returned to the parents, he was astonished to find a baby far from dead, but one that was fully alive and responsive. It seemed a miracle.

Counted among the most marvelous miracles of the Torah is the splitting of the Red Sea. The Children of Israel are described as having been convinced of the power of God, and more importantly in the existence of God, with this miracle: "...Israel saw the Egyptians dead on the seashore. And when Israel saw the awesome power which the Lord wielded against the Egyptians, the people feared the Lord; they had faith in the Lord and His servant Moses."[29] This is a perfect example of seeing is believing.

Finally, the most publicized miracle of the Jewish people is the one pertaining to Hanukkah. This story, which takes place in the second century BCE, recalls a battle pitting Judeans against the dominant reigning force of the day, the Syrian Greeks. The battle was fought over both religion and culture, the one side trying to force the dominant culture of the day,

---

29   Exodus 14:30-31

a Hellenistic culture, on the Judeans. In this way, Hellenism would both predominate and replace the local religious and cultural norms. The Judeans resisted and against all odds, won, an outstanding victory considering the overwhelming force of the Syrians. The Maccabees (for so the fighting Judeans were known) retook the ancient Temple that had been defiled by the Syrians' Hellenistic practices—the erection of idols, the worship of the gods, and the sacrifice of unauthorized and unkosher animals, like swine. They sought to cleanse the Temple environs of its impurities and rekindle the menorah. They found kosher oil sufficient for one day's worth of light, yet according to the tradition, it burned for eight full days. A miracle!

In spite of this Jewish story, and many other biblical attestations to miracles, modern-day struggles with Judaism often focus on these events which are framed as history but sound more like they belong in the fantasy file. Contemporary explanations almost never depend on the miraculous as the basis for what has transpired, and as such, the miracles of the past are met with great skepticism and suspicion. The ambivalence of the Jewish community with present-day miracles is beautifully illustrated by a Talmudic story revolving around the holiday of Purim. Purim is a happy day of gift-giving, feasting, and drinking. Although these days the drinking dimension is played down, all for good reason, there are still those who happily down the *"L'hayyim's"* until their cognitive faculties go fuzzy over the distinction between blessed Mordecai (hero of the Book of Esther, ritually read on Purim) and accursed Haman (villain of the Book of Esther). And so the Talmud relates the story of two rabbis, Rabbah and Rav Zeira, who enthusiastically fulfill the mitzvah of boozing up, to the point where Rabbah rises up and murders Rav Zeira. The next morning, guilty as the man holding the blood-dripping knife at the crime scene, Rabbah fervently prays to God on behalf of his dead colleague, and miraculously, God restores Rav Zeira to life. The following year, Rabbah once again invites Rav Zeira to the customary Purim feast, the bar fully stocked. Rav Zeira declines. Would anyone blame him? As Rav Zeira explains to his boozing bosom buddy, "miracles don't always happen."[30] This was Rav Zeira's way of saying, past performance is not indicative of future results, sobering words from a man with experience and, by this time, elevated risk-aversion.

But are any of the preceding examples truly miracles, episodes of divine intervention in a world that otherwise is hostage to a morality-indifferent nature? One might as easily explain the drowning of the Egyptians as due to some unknown natural phenomenon that caught the Egyptians by surprise, or the possibility that Rav Zeira's resurrection was not from death but from extreme hangover, or that the Maccabees were great warriors but horrible physicists, misunderstanding the potential energy in that little jug of oil. These are stories that are told from one generation to the next and remain popular, even for those who might erase the mystery of the miracle via a reasonable though unproven explanation.

---

30   Megillah 7b

Absent a scientific explanation, the ancients resorted to their own fanciful reasoning of what otherwise would be a natural phenomenon, as for example, Moses at the burning bush. The burning bush seemed to burn without end and it is at this conflagration that Moses first encounters God. God instructs Moses to return to Egypt to initiate the liberation of the Israelites. Can there be any scientific explanation for a bush that burns without end? Some have suggested there is. The bush could possibly have been a concentration of several common desert plants known as acacia. Acacia is a good source of charcoal which allows for lengthy burns. Given the heat of the desert sun above or the possibility that the plants sat atop volcanic activity from below, or both, spontaneous combustion is plausible. The idea that Mount Sinai, which is identified as the burning bush's location,[31] was an active volcano could explain the smoke, the fire, and its violent trembling during Moses' delivery of the Ten Commandments. On top of all this, Benny Shanon, Professor Emeritus of Psychology at Hebrew University, has determined that the acacia plant bears within it ayahuasca, a hallucinogen, and that Moses may very well have been tripping during his "alleged" encounter with God.[32]

Another example of the miraculous would be the falling of manna from heaven, a daily occurrence (except on Shabbat) and a substance that nourished the Israelites throughout their forty years of roaming the wilderness. They never went hungry

---

31   See Exodus 3:1

32   Jeffay, Nathan. "Moses Saw God Because he was Stoned—Again." *https://www. theguardian.com/world/2008/mar/06/religion.israelandthepalestinians,* The Guardian, March 5, 2008. Accessed: February 25, 2018.

due to this spiritual food that God delivered to them. But could there be some scientific explanation behind it all? Again, some have suggested there is. Dibyajyoti Lahiri has suggested that manna was trehalose, a sweet, crystalline carbohydrate, the product of multiple organisms, like fungo or bacteria, and a parasitic beetle called the Trehala manna (named after the biblical manna). The cocoons of these beetles, readily found in the Middle East, are nutritious in both proteins and carbohydrates. And the Bedouin are known to use it today as a sweetner.[33]

The presumption of scientific explanations for biblical miracles is that if our ancestors only knew what we know, they would never have had to resort to supernatural explanations. In debunking the miraculous explanations for these events, one could argue that these exercises in disillusionment are positive in order to keep people from believing in biblical fairy tales. But a negative predisposition to religion or the Bible may lay at the heart of these scientific assaults on biblical narratives. As explained earlier (see chapter 2 on the Bible), the sacred literature is not a book of science. To undermine it on the basis of science is like dismissing Harry Potter tales since everyone knows that magic is spurious.

Every time science further examines the Bible with a scalpel, it eviscerates both the power and point of the narrative. Moses' encounter with God at the burning bush establishes his mission to confront Pharaoh and free the Israelites as a matter of divine significance. Moses' mission was not merely a political

---

33   Six Scientific Explanations for Famous 'Bible Miracles,' Cracked.com, June 5, 2016

or social action, but a deeply spiritual and religious campaign. God rejects the idea of man-gods, whom Pharaoh, in the eyes of his Egyptian subjects, was. To confront and ultimately smash the idolatry of this world, which so often results in the subjugation of others is a mission that is, like the burning bush, unending. As for the manna which science could simply identify as natural Bedouin sugar, the point there is that the Israelites were sustained not by physical nutrition but by something spiritual. "Fresh Direct," but from God and not a grocer, from heaven and not from the earth. This was God's way of growing a nation of priests fed on kosher ambrosia, the food of the God of Israel.

Absent scientific explanations, our biblical ancestors explained natural phenomena as the work of supernatural forces. So what? Moderns may know better but the ancients did not. In ascribing the inexplicable to forces that were both beyond yet benign, our ancestors gained relief from their anxieties. Our Jewish ancestors understood the rainbow as a sign that God would no longer destroy the world by a devastating flood. It most assuredly is not that, but what a beautiful way to bring closure to all the fears that a world-wide devastating deluge generates.

More important than the relief that a miraculous explanation may effect is the intimacy it creates between the believer and God. The miracle, when so identified, is the greatest antidote to existential loneliness that exists. The miracle is the opposite of a world in which there is no God, no justice, no compassion, and ultimately, no meaning. To view an event as the result of a God who will not allow a tragedy to transpire or disaster to dominate means that we do live in a world of compassion and love, a world in which our every decision and action unfolds under the watchful eye of a protective God, a cosmic parent who would never allow harm to mar God's children. The biblical Chronicler understood this *hashgahah p'ratit,* God's "personal oversight" of each and every individual when a paean to God is quoted as composed by the chief Levite at the time of King David's reign (circa 1000 BCE):

> O offspring of Israel, His servant, O descendants of Jacob, His chosen ones. He is the Lord our God; His judgments are throughout the earth. Be mindful of His covenant forever, the word He gave for a thousand generations, that He made with Abraham, swore to Isaac, and confirmed in a statute for Jacob, for Israel, an eternal covenant, saying, "To you, I will give the land of Canaan as your allotted heritage." You were then few in number, of little account, merely sojourning there, wandering from nation to nation, from one kingdom to another. He allowed no one to oppress them; He rebuked kings on their account, "Do not touch My anointed ones; do not harm My prophets."[34]

To feel with one's full heart that God is there to protect from all danger and disease, from all mishap and accident, is a

---

34   I Chronicles 16:13-22

tremendous high. And yet, the identification of miracles is so often accompanied by a dark side, and one that can only generate disillusionment if not anger. It may be a miracle for that one person to survive a plane crash, but it is no miracle for the other ten who lost their lives. It may be a miracle for the cancer patient to go into remission, but it is no miracle for hundreds of others who succumb to the disease. It may be a miracle for so many Jews throughout the generations who escaped the executioner's sword, but it was no miracle for the millions who did not. We delight in the "miracles" that happen, while ignoring the miracles that never materialize. It is much the same with gamblers who tell of their wins, but never of their substantial losses. The victories are so much more enchanting. And then there is the great spoiler, Science, ever ready to explain away the miracle. Science is the party-pooper of the imagination, leaving us with no more than dumb luck, a cold and disinterested universe, in which happiness belongs to the lucky, not the loved. Rationalists abhor the miraculous—it's all explainable, it's all good fortune, and it's never divine. And so the question that any rational-minded Jew might ask is this: Is it still possible to believe in the miraculous without abdicating the very foundation of modernity, which would be a solid alliance with reason?

Abraham Joshua Heschel (1907-1972), one of the leading Jewish theologians of the twentieth century, wrote, "Mankind will not perish for want of information; but only for want of appreciation. The beginning of our happiness lies in the understanding that life without wonder is not worth living. What we lack is not a will to believe but a will to wonder."[35] Heschel's thought here is part of a larger principle which he referred to as "radical amazement." Radical amazement was his term for seeing the extraordinary in the ordinary. What we see daily, routinely, perhaps endlessly, and thus that which is perceived as "ordinary," simply is not. With an appreciation for radical amazement comes a world that is transformed by wonder and thus full of miracles.

I rarely give much attention to the desk at which I sit, but were I to contemplate its construction for just a few moments, I would have reason for amazement. It has now held up over eighteen years and endured coffee and soda spills, falling staplers, and inadvertent scratches from letter openers and scissors. It supports a computer, printer, two speakers, a telephone, a solar lamp and a hutch that itself bears the weight of heavy tomes, old cameras, paper supplies and an assortment of empty whiskey bottles (I collect—the bottle shape and labelling are deliciously artistic). The desk is not rectangular but carefully rounded with no rough edges, a finish revealing its wooden grain though protected by some laminate that makes it resistant to stain and fading. I sit at this desk with rarely a thought of the many hours invested into its design, its construction, or the hours involved by lumberjacks harvesting the wood, or the years it took to grow the tree from which the desk was built. As a believer, the construction of the desk might lead me to ponder the planet on which we all live, where the tree

---

35   Abraham Joshua Heschel, God in Search of Man (New York: Farrar, Straus & Giroux, 1955), p.46

for wood grew; the tree whose seed was planted by no human hand, but whose woody product nonetheless ended up as a desk, in my study. It is in the contemplation of all that went into the fashioning of this "ordinary" object that its extraordinary nature is exposed. Given its design and construction, I should be radically amazed. We all should.

One of the great illusions of our lives is the night sky, an orb sporting a host of twinkling, iridescent points of light that would appear no further from us than the jet airliner streaming overhead, flashing its own set of lights. But as science has taught us, those tiny shimmering's in the firmament are not so nearby. Beyond our own sun, the closest star system to us is Alpha Centauri, a three-star system, the closest of the three stars being Proxima Centauri, which is approximately 4.22 light years from the earth. If humans ever wanted to visit Proxima Centauri, their estimated arrival would be 4.22 years from the time of departure, but this only if traveling at the speed of light, which for humans is not possible—at least not yet. So the closest star shining in our night time sky is 24,790,819,060,507.32 miles away, which is rounded off to 25 trillion miles. It's understandable why measurements in light years is preferable. But among the stars that shine in the night time sky are those that are far more than 4.22 light years away. Consider Table 1, recording distances of the stars from earth, in light years:

STAR	DISTANCE IN LIGHT YEARS
Sirius	8.6
Vega	25
Arcturus	34
Canopus	74
Archernar	139
Rigel	860
Betelgeuse	1,500

Table 1

Looking at the night time sky is testimony to what the stars looked like years ago, actually light years ago. In looking at Betelgeuse, it is not seen as it shines today, but as it shined 1500 years ago, in approximately the sixth century. The heavens above us presumably testify to the present, but in fact present a living map of the past.

Earth resides in a solar system that is part of a spiral galaxy known as the Milky Way. The measure of the full length of the Milky Way, from one end to the other, is about 100,000 light years. That's a big galaxy, but hardly the biggest galaxy in the universe. In Table 2, consider the lengths of other known galaxies, again measured in light years:

GALAXY	LENGTH IN LIGHT YEARS
Cartwheel Galaxy	130,000
Andromeda Galaxy	220,000
MGC	490,000
NGC6872	522,000
M87	980,000
Coma B	1,000,000
Hercules A	1.5 million

Table 2

Scientists estimate an approximate 100 billion galaxies within our universe and the light of billions of these stars will never be seen by human eyes. Their distance from earth is so far their light has yet to reach our eyes. The average height of an American male is about 5'10" and of the American female, 5' 4". Given the scale of the universe, we would overestimate our own size were we to describe ourselves as mere specks of dust. We are far smaller than that. And yet, these fractional specks of dust have been given the ability to actually measure the dimensions of the universe and as such ponder its mysteries and majesties, as well as stand in awe of the human capacity to capture it all. It is in the contemplation of this "ordinary" thing called the night sky, that we begin to realize the extraordinary nature of the universe in which we live and our place within it.

Human eyes do not merely look outward to the heavens, but have dared to look inward, into the very mechanics of a human body. There are an estimated 30-40 trillion cells in the average human body, each with a specific function, designed to cooperate and collaborate with one another in order to create and maintain a functioning human being. It is as if the human body were itself a major corporation with 30-40 trillion employees, each following its job description with great allegiance and dependability. The cells of our body function 24/7 with few demands save proper nutrition and exercise. They work tirelessly and remain unacknowledged until for some reason, they act up, as they might with a security breach, an unwelcomed stranger (a pathogen) having entered the firm.

The importance of cells is most acknowledged when they are no longer functioning as they should, but the overwhelming general experience is that they typically do what they have been designed to do. It is in the contemplation of this "ordinary" thing called the human body that we begin to realize its complex and extraordinary nature, and how it continues to function in both waking and sleeping hours.

But does any of this qualify as a miracle?

If a miracle must be a supernatural event, then the desk, the universe, and the human body themselves are in no way miraculous. Each can be analyzed and broken down into component parts that can be explained—and it is understood that with the passage of time, the knowledge base explaining all that is will expand. But if a miracle is that which connects a human being with God in a moment of theological clarity, a sudden and deep appreciation, an instant of radical amazement, then it is virtually impossible to take a single step anywhere without an encounter of the miraculous. Oddly enough, the term miracle is derived from the Latin *mirari*, meaning "to wonder." The supernatural may be fascinating, but the natural no less. And because understanding the natural world requires no suspension of reason, it may be said that its appreciation is even more fascinating. It is for this reason that the Jewish morning begins with a blessing in which we acknowledge the extraordinary in the ordinary. The cock crows. Amazing! And that's just the beginning of a day that will be filled with endless moments of Godly encounters, each and every one, radically amazing, each and every one, a miracle in its own way.

• • • • •

TO THE MIRACLE SKEPTIC

Miracles exist, but they needn't be phenomena that defy human reason. We need only to let loose our wonder in the ordinary to see the extraordinary, and allow for radical amazement in the possible, without resort to fascination with the impossible.

8 THE AFTER-LIFE SKEPTIC

When I die, that's it. Or is it?

Lee Adler, a member of my congregation in Springfield, NJ, at the time known as Temple Beth Ahm, was a kind soul, a brilliant PhD, and like many a good husband, not particularly responsive to his wife's requests for replacing burnt-out lightbulbs. Lee's wife, Alice, told me the lightbulb story. She had been urging Lee to change a lightbulb in the bathroom for several months. It just wasn't happening. Lee was a conscientious employee and would get to work early. He worked for a division of Cantor Fitzgerald, the financial services firm, and was on the 103rd story of the World Trade Center on 9/11. He never made it out of the building and his body was never found. After six months of Alice asking her husband to please change the inoperative lightbulb in the bathroom, on 9/12, the bulb turned on spontaneously. Hearing Alice tell the story, Alice's sister-in-law, Randi, confided that in days following 9/11, her outdoor motion-detector light would turn on for no apparent reason.

Both of them believed that it was Lee's way of letting them know, and the rest of the family, that he was okay.

The question, "Is there life after death?" is a question asked with both curiosity and anxiety. One could also ask "Is there life before birth?" under the assumption that if humans have souls, and souls are eternal, then life is merely an eruption of daylight between two nights, the darkness before birth and the darkness after death. But it is the "Is there life after death?" question whose tenacity is the more unrelenting and the one that most preoccupies the imaginations of the living. Having knowledge of a beginning in birth, humans are naturally predisposed to wonder about the ending: death. And the most persistent question in this regard is about continuity: Is death the end, or is there something more? Is death the beginning of something new and different? Having been born and presumably conscious during one's lifetime, it's difficult to conceive of the whole of experience vanishing into nothingness, as if one had never been born. It's jarring. None of us are too pleased with the foreknowledge of death, particularly our own. But it is this very phenomenon that has given rise to the deepest of all philosophical questions. The fact of human mortality, our knowledge that our own lives will come to an end, may be the ultimate question of all philosophical discourse.

Over the years, Judaism has evolved into a this-worldly tradition rather than an other-worldly tradition. Jews rarely talk seriously about heaven or hell, and when they do, it's usually a reference to a Viennese Table (heaven) or a broken air-conditioner in July (hell). Nonetheless, the traditional literature does touch on issues of both heaven and hell, and these sources teach us much about the Jewish conceptions of the afterlife.

The closest concept Jews have in regard to what people typically refer to as heaven would be the *olam haba,* literally, the world-to-come. It stands in contrast with the *olam hazeh* or this world. But even in the case of the *olam haba,* its exact meaning is anything but exact. Sometimes it refers to that period of time when all the dead are resurrected and brought back to life, or a time of the immortality of all souls, or—and this would be the sense closest to the idea of heaven—that period immediately following death when the dead enter into some celestial paradise and bask in the glory of God. One of the most popular works of Jewish ethics is Pirkei Avot, which begins with the following words of comfort: "Every Israelite has a share in the *olam haba,* as is stated, 'And your people, all of them righteous, shall possess the land for all time; they are the shoot that I planted, My handiwork in which I glory.'"[36] This is a pretty good deal, as all of Israel become future heirs of this blessed *olam haba.* But the gift is not necessarily a free admission ticket to heaven, as the accompanying words of Isaiah seem to position a kind of Righteousness Bouncer just outside the heavenly entrance. Israel enters because of its righteousness, but what if an Israelite isn't so righteous or pious? Do sinning Israelites also receive heaven's complimentary pass?

---

36   Pirkei Avot 1:1; the recorded prooftext taken from Isaiah 60:21

On this matter, the rabbis were not so generous. They cite any number of Israelites who lose their share in the next world due to their indiscretions in this one. Among those who lose out are:

1. One who claims that the resurrection of the dead is not found in the Torah;
2. One who says that the Torah is not a product of heaven;
3. One who follows the Greek philosopher, Epicurus;
4. Anyone who chants over a wound the following incantation—"...I will not bring upon you any of the diseases that I brought upon the Egyptians, for I am the Lord, your healer;"[37]
5. The following three kings—Jeroboam, Ahab, and Menasseh;
6. One who attempts to pronounce the Divine name (YHVH).[38]

Clearly, this list of no-no's was a technique, and probably a very effective one, in promulgating those beliefs or actions that the rabbis found particularly objectionable. The last thing one would ever want is to find their name on a royal list of kings who were booted out of heaven. So where do all these bad pomegranates go?

The closest concept Jews have in regard to what people typically refer to as hell would be *Gehenna,* a term that follows a Greek rendering of the original Hebrew, *Gei Ben-hinnom,*

---

37   Exodus 15:26

38   Sanhedrin 90a

literally, the Valley of the Son of Hinom. *Gei Ben-hinom* is a valley in Jerusalem with an egregious reputation:

> For the people of Judah have done what displeases Me—declares the Lord. They have set up their abominations in the house which is called by My name (i.e., the Jerusalem Temple), and have defiled it. And they have built the shrines of Topheth (unclear what Topheth is but the presumption is that it is of Canaanite origin and connected with child sacrifice) in the Valley of Ben-hinnom to burn their sons and daughters in fire—which I did not command, which never crossed My mind.[39]

If ever there was a clear provenance for a fiery hell, it would come from the Hebrew *Gehenna* where the valley fires burned children alive in some horrific pagan ritual. *Gehenna* therefore begins as a physical place, a valley of horror, its fiery metaphysical counterpart evolving only later, particularly among Christians. This stands in contrast with *olam haba*, a metaphysical concept with no physical counterpart. There is no physical utopia, no valley or community free of strife or sorrow, that exists. The Garden of Eden, which is more of a mindset than a physical location, serves as no exception, as humans are banished from Eden forever. In any event, dead sinners would not necessarily be sent off to *Gehenna*, but more dramatically lose out on their share of *olam haba*. On this earth,

---

39   Jeremiah 7:30-31

they have experienced no peace for it does not exist, and the peace which does exist after death, they are denied. The rabbis provided good reasons for anyone with a conscience to repent of their sins.

The Torah assumes that the dead are not necessarily gone. But to the extent that they are dead, they should not be consulted. And so the Torah instructs as follows: "Do not turn to ghosts and do not inquire of familiar spirits, to be defiled by them: I am the Lord your God."[40] The idea here is to not conjure up the "ghosts" of loved ones who have passed, otherwise known as, "familiar spirits." It is not exactly clear what the Torah means by its concern with defilement, but whatever it is, it isn't good. At the same time, the Torah clearly regards this conjuring of the dead as a possibility since it rules against it. It even records a séance of sorts.

The story revolves around King Saul, the first king of Israel. Saul was a tortured soul, having fallen out of the good graces of his mentor, the prophet Samuel; forever challenged by warring tribes like the Philistines; disappointed in his son, Jonathan; and particularly paranoid of a young and popular warrior-poet by the name of David, the very same David who someday would be king. Faced with yet another military challenge by the Philistines, and unsure how to respond strategically to this most recent threat, he seeks out a medium who might draw the dead prophet Samuel up from the grave to give him the necessary guidance and courage which he, at that

---

40   Leviticus 19:31

time, so desperately needs. His servants find that medium in a woman who resided in En-Dor. As the prohibition against consultation with the dead was well-known, Saul dresses in disguise. He meets the woman, requests her services, but she, aware of the law, resists. She knows the rules and desires no trouble, but Saul assures her safety. When Saul reveals that the ghost he wishes to consult is none other than the prophet Samuel, the woman recognizes her king and complies with his wishes. She effectively conjures up the ghost of Samuel as her reputation would have her do, but the meeting does not go well. The prophet is upset with having been disturbed from his eternal rest, reiterates God's displeasure with Saul, and ends by predicting a Philistine victory over Israel and the imminent death of Saul and his sons. Soon thereafter, the Philistines do summarily defeat the Israelites, and Saul, in a fit of despair, commits suicide rather than fall by the sword of the enemy. This is the sort of biblical story that generates all sorts of questions about the nature of the biblical narrative. Is it history? Is it fantasy? Is it a combination of both? However one may understand the biblical text, this is a narrative that speaks to a people who find life after death credible.

Mikey was one of the spirited, kind, and fun-loving kids that every Religious School teacher adores. He worked to the best of his abilities and always wanted to please, always wanted to do the right thing. At the age of 15, while jogging with his high school track team, he was hit by a speeding car. He lingered only a few days in the hospital after which he succumbed to his injuries. We sent him to his eternal rest with a funeral attended by well over 800 members of the community. Sometime later, his mother confided in me that she had consulted with mediums to see if she could connect with her Mikey. At one such meeting, without her so much as saying anything to the medium about why she was present, the medium knew that it was about the loss of a child, that it was an accident that took his life, and that there was a woman in the audience who had a photo of Mikey in her wallet (later found to be true). While attending another session, a medium told her that Mikey wanted her to stop pursuing him. She has since suspended her visits to mediums or trying to connect with Mikey.

The interest in life after death may stem from our broken hearts or from that existential concern over the fleeting nature of our mortal selves. It also serves as an answer to the particularly disturbing theological question of theodicy. Theodicy, very simply, is the question of why the righteous suffer while the wicked prosper. When our biblical ancestors posited a world controlled by a single God, and that God was also an ethical and moral God, they nevertheless were stuck with the annoying reality that sometimes good people are beset by painful unjust circumstances. People within the community who may be the first to comfort the sick, help the disabled, volunteer to assist in some building project, cook for the hungry, cheer up the depressed, etc., may also be the very same people whose house burns down, or are robbed, or lose all their money, or witness the death of a child, or become deathly ill, etc. It all seems like a punishment and in a just world run by a just God, it just shouldn't happen. Yet it does. One of the solutions to this glitch in the theology of monotheism is to posit life after death. On this basis, one can honestly acknowledge the suffering of the righteous and the injustice of it all, without impugning God's goodness. Sorrow may be a feature of the *olam hazeh,* this world, but in the *olam haba,* the world-to-come, all is corrected (more on Theodicy in chapter 9).

Still, the rabbis did not portray the *olam haba* as a rock and rollin' palace of pleasure: "In the *olam haba,* there is no eating or drinking, no sexual intimacy, business, jealousy, hatred, or competition, but the righteous sit with their crowns on their heads feasting on the brilliance of the Divine Presence."[41] Who could blame the righteous for raising objections to this so-called reward? By the same token, the rabbis were not ascetics, and encouraged people to take advantage of the pleasures of this world, even assuming that in the *olam haba,* candidates will have to give an accounting before the Master of the Universe for every legitimate pleasure they denied themselves in this world.[42] In other words, tough as this world can be, it is in this world where pleasure is accessible. The world-to-come will not be unpleasant, but as a place of intangibility and perfect tranquility, the pleasures are of a *sui generis* order. Judging from the horrific acts of Islamic terrorists, murdering others and killing themselves with promises of fleshy pleasures

---

41   Berakhot 17a

42   Jerusalem Talmud, Kiddushin 4:12

in an immaterial world, there is great utilitarian wisdom in the spiritual doldrums of the Jewish *olam haba.* If you're out to get the gold, best seek it out in this world, for in the world-to-come, it won't be worth much, if it exists at all.

The number of times that those of this world have experienced some sort of connection with those of the world-to-come suggests two domains that are not distinct one from the other, but in some way overlap or comingle with each other. The rabbis of old knew of this connection when linking the two worlds via a "prozdor," or vestibule. "Rabbi Jacob states, '*Olam hazeh* is comparable to a vestibule before the *olam haba.* Prepare yourself in the vestibule that you may enter the banquet hall,'"[43] the banquet hall a metaphor for the *olam haba.* One can almost sense, as apparently Rabbi Jacob does, the proximity of the *olam haba* to *the olam hazeh.* One could stroll down a relatively short corridor and knock on the doors of heaven and possibly enter, though the rabbi does not go that far nor does he instruct anyone else to do so.

In 2008, Eben Alexander experienced what has become known as a near-death experience or an NDE. Due to an acute case of meningitis, he went into a coma for seven days during which his cerebral cortex was under attack and not functioning. When he finally emerged from the coma he told of an experience which was akin to his having visited heaven, with reassurances that he would soon return to the land of the living. What makes Alexander's account unique is the fact that he is himself

---

43   Pirkei Avot 4:21

a neurosurgeon, capable of analyzing his experience from a more scientific perspective. He is convinced that heaven is real, citing his experience as empirical proof. He wrote of the experience in *Proof of Heaven: A Neurosurgeon's Journey into the Afterlife.* His testimony, however, was not above dispute and some reputable scientists have questioned both his account of the experience and his conclusions which do not take all possibilities into consideration. Then again, his account is one among many accounts, so often characterized by encounters with angelic figures, peace, tranquility, and reassurances of a return to their loved ones on earth sweet earth.

The intersection between the tangible and the intangible, the physical and the metaphysical, does have a New Age ring to it, but it is not substantially different from a reality we experience all the time. In fact, our experience of reality is a rather cerebral, intangible event itself. We perceive reality as we do because our bodily receptors—eyes, ears, nose, tongue, fingers—allow us to perceive that reality in a specific way. And whatever data these receptors gather via light waves, sound waves, odors, taste, and touch are mediated via a specific instrument, the human brain. This most complex organ of the entire body allows us to perceive the outside with synaptic speed that takes place wholly on the inside. Our experience of the external is modulated by the experience of the internal. A brief foray into science fiction may further illustrate the point.

Say an extra-terrestrial being (ETB) landed on earth and began to examine the world as we know it, but via the only way

it could know us, with its ETB brain or whatever correspond-
ing mechanism it had to decipher such matters. It could easily
be argued that for the ETB, because of the construction of its
brain, colors would not be perceived as we perceive them, nor
sounds, nor tastes, nor fragrances. This is because we and the
ETB can perceive the world only to the extent that our respective brains permit us, and different brains will perceive the world
in different ways. Our understanding of the outside is limited
to the parameters set by the inside. How we experience each
other holds profound implications for life after death because
memory can reproduce the very images, sounds, tastes, and
perhaps even the feel and fragrance of the other, just as the
other was, even without that person's living presence. And
what goes on within the brain when those memories are triggered after death is essentially no less real than when the brain
is triggered by the person who physically stands before us. In
this way, the living have a way of keeping the dead alive—in
effect, an afterlife phenomenon.

I was once handed a dollar bill by a grieving daughter.
The bill belonged to her mother. "Smell," she said. The dollar
bore the fragrance of perfume. And with a wistful tear making
its way down her cheek she said, "That's my mother," a woman
with the unique habit of perfuming the dollars before distribut-
ing them to the children and grandchildren. One might counter
with the fact that her perception is not life after death, rather
perfume. Yet it is perfume, a specific perfume, a fragrance that
triggered a whole set of memories for this grieving woman

whose experience of her mother was so real that it moved her to tears.

In speaking of loved ones who have passed on, we will often say, *zikhronam l'vrakhah*—May their memory bring blessings. And so it is that we hope that the memories triggered are ones that generate a contentment or happiness, a state of grateful resignation that may be described as blessed. To the extent that life after death is in part a function of the memory of those who remain alive, what about those living whom we would prefer to forget? Perhaps the memory of a loved one conjures up a whole host of unpleasant, perhaps even painful memories—mental, physical, or verbal abuses, whatever they may be, and the living decide that forgetting the source of pain is the preferred and just response. This happens all the time. Frankly, it would be difficult, if not totally foolish, to demand that the wounded living treat dead abusers magnanimously. The decision to forget, to erase, is sometimes evidence of a healthy resistance, a sort of therapeutic vengeance that breeds satisfaction without harming another. It is in this way that a victim may deny the perpetrator's share in the *olam haba,* as is deserved. When the Torah instructs the Jewish people to "blot out the memory of Amalek from under heaven,"[44] it is essentially a damning of the unworthy. Deny them life after death by denying them a space in your memory. Forget about them for they do not deserve a share in the *olam haba.* This is a lesson for everyone. We should be careful to live life in such a way

---

44   Deuteronomy 25:19

that those closest to us prefer to remember our memory and not erase it.

This issue leads to yet another dimension of the Jewish conception of life after death and that is for whom it is reserved—Jews alone or non-Jews as well? Rabbi Eliezer and Rabbi Joshua debate this very issue as to whether the *olam haba* is reserved for the Jewish faithful or more broadly for any person who has lived a commendable life. Rabbi Joshua noted that all the righteous of the world hold a share in the *olam haba.*[45] It is one's goodness, not one's faith, that secures the entrance key to the *olam haba.* This too comports well with the living who play an essential role in the continuing life of the dead. When one lives life in such a way as to make a positive impact on another, that impact does not dissipate with death. When loved ones keep us in their memory, they resurrect our souls, even after our deaths.

The Talmud offers a glimpse into what the *olam haba* must be like by comparing it to three experiences: a sunny day, the observance of Shabbat, and sexual intercourse.[46] One could, I suppose, write a book deliberating over a common denominator between these three: *Sex on a Sunny Sabbath: The Search for Heaven.* But the rabbis, always witty, must have had something in mind when they zeroed in on these three sensuous experiences. Perhaps their thinking involves answers to the

---

45   Tosefta Sanhedrin 13:2

46   Berakhot 57b

fears people express about death itself, about consignment to the grave.

Will it be cold? No, not at all. Technically freed from our sense receptors, in death there should be no sensation of pain or cold. But this should not be taken as a state of oblivion. Were it to be compared to anything at all, it will be most like a sunny day, pleasant and carefree.

Will it be lonely? No, not at all. It will be more like Shabbat, when family specifically gathers to celebrate with each other. In death, there is no longing, for in death we are closest to the source of all life, God. In the next world therefore there is no loneliness.

Will it be passionless? No not at all. There will be an intense intimacy of souls united with each other and souls united with God. There are many literary parallels drawn between sexual passion and spiritual fervor. This metaphor calls attention to the intensity of one's relationship with God. The afterlife is characterized by such spiritual highs.

In short, the Talmudic dictum on what the *olam haba* is like is a fleshing out of a verse in Psalms: "For You will not give me up to Sheol (the grave), or let Your faithful set eyes on the Pit,"[47] "the Pit" a reference to the Bible's murky and ill-defined place where the spirits of the dead reside. I have often comforted the grieving with reassurances that though a loved one has been buried, a soul has been liberated and united with God. I can't prove it. I can't swear by it. The mourners probably know

---

47   Psalm 16:10

that there is no proof of it. But for all its rational decrepitude, it brings comfort. At a time of sorrow, comfort is what people need, and my objective is to deliver it.

When I came to Midway Jewish Center in 1999, I had the pleasure and honor of working with Moish Dubinsky, a very talented and devoted cantor who had long served the congregation but who was fated to pass away only a few years into my tenure. I officiated at his unveiling at which time his widow, Ellen Dubinsky, told the following story. She said that before his death, Moish assured her that he would send her signs indicating that all was well in the next world. After his death, she did receive such signs which she understood as having been sent from her husband, and she described those heart-stopping moments. One sign in particular was of special significance to her. It was July and she was returning home from a camp job in order to attend the closing on her new home. She had not sensed Moish's presence for some time and feeling anxious about emergent transitions, she prayed in her car for some reassuring sign. Within a matter of seconds, a flock of birds flew before her car, appearing as if it were from out of nowhere. She immediately knew this was a sign from her beloved. Ellen told this story during the unveiling at the cemetery, and those of us gathered looked at her as she looked at us. The moment she concluded her story about the flock of birds, hundreds of birds appeared behind her, materializing as if out of the earth, and rose in flight. We were literally dumbfounded. She was facing us, and could not have seen the birds suddenly rise, but she saw from the expressions on our faces that something unusual had happened. Indeed, something very unusual had happened.

And there you have it. Just at the point of thinking rationally about all of life, and feeling pretty good about it, a flock of birds takes flight, at just the right time, and in the right place. A divine monkey wrench has been cast from the heavens above to the earth below, God's way of saying, "Hey—you know what you know, and I know what you know, and then there's 99.9999% of all the rest of knowledge in the universe, which you do not know. Don't get too cocky!"

· · · · ·

TO THE AFTERLIFE SKEPTIC

Death cannot end a life well-lived. The loved ones we leave behind reconstitute us in their minds, repeatedly. And however poor our memories may be, God never forgets.

9 THE GOD-IS-GOOD SKEPTIC

I won't believe in a God that would allow my child, or any other child, to die.

Art was in his early sixties, a very even-tempered and kindly fellow who had recently retired after a full and satisfying career teaching high school. He raised, together with his wife of over thirty years, a beautiful and successful daughter. He had no mortgage on his house and was toying with the idea of moving down to Florida, enjoying the sun, the ocean, and a little bit of fishing too. And then the news came. He was diagnosed with pancreatic cancer and both the nature of the cancer together with its late discovery led doctors to believe that his condition was unlikely to respond favorably to any known therapies. He had, at best, only six more months to live. Art told me all this during a meeting he scheduled soon after the diagnosis, in his typically stoic manner, and in a concerted attempt to put his house in order. He wanted to be sure I was available to officiate at his funeral, wanted to know of any customs surrounding his death and burial of which he should be aware, confided in me about some concerns he had for his wife, and wanted to keep the whole thing relatively quiet within the community. This was a man with a keen sense of responsibility. Six months later, almost to the day, he died.

Izzy, a young man in his thirties, showed up regularly at Friday night services. He was a quiet guy with a beautiful smile, a businessman who loved his job and his family back in Israel. The percentage of young single men regularly attending a suburban synagogue is not very high, so Izzy stood out. The other congregants, most of them much older than he, adored him like a son. He told me good news about his forthcoming marriage to a lovely woman who had grown up in the synagogue, Shomrei Emunah in Montclair, NJ. The two married, had a child, and when the little girl was about three months of age, Izzy was killed in a car accident. A driver ran a stop sign and hit Izzy's car directly where he sat. He was killed almost instantly.

Life seems not to care much for personal plans. Every family can tell a tale of an uncle or a grandparent or a cousin whose life was disrupted because of broken promises, theft, fire, disease, a murder, an infidelity, a war, etc. And whatever the story, it never seems fair. Our little blue planet is not an easy place to live on, and sooner or later, all of us will encounter what can only be described as the garbage of life: injustice, cruelty, or painful absurdity. It is essentially inevitable. And, of course, for the Jewish people, perhaps for all of Western civilization, the most egregious example of inhumanity would be the Shoah or Holocaust itself, the systematic murder of six million Jews at the hands of Nazis, including 1.5 million children. It is a human tragedy of inconceivable magnitude.

One of the thorniest and persistent questions about any variation on ethical monotheistic theology is why the righteous suffer while the wicked prosper. This is a classical framing of the question, a formula that is deliberately exaggerated in order to clearly illustrate the injustice of it all. The real issue at hand is not so much the righteous versus the wicked as much as it is about common folk who deserve better versus the unworthy who benefit beyond their due. The paradox lies in this: If the God we believe in is truly good, then how can such a good God either punish directly or allow others or other circumstances to create punishing conditions for those who deserve better? And if God is truly just, then how can such a just God allow the undeserving to enjoy benefits that by right they ought to be denied? Some have claimed that the answer to this paradox is simple: God is neither good nor just. But if that is the answer, how then is that not a contradiction to all that ethical monotheism purports to be? This, as one might well imagine, is hardly a contemporary question. It is a question that the ancients struggled with almost from the very inception of monotheistic belief.

One answer of the rabbis was to see suffering not as a punishment, but rather as a divine gift. They found proof for this counter-intuitive proposition in the words of Isaiah 53:10, which reads: "But the Lord chose to crush him by disease, that, if he so sacrificed himself, he might see offspring and have long life, and that through him, the Lord's purpose might prosper."[48] The Talmudic passage that interprets this verse basically frames suffering as a divine challenge, befalling those whom God loves in order to test them. The test will be whether the individual will have the presence of mind and strength of heart to accept the suffering not only sans complaint, but also with an open heart, willingly and happily. And if the sufferer passes the test, the reward will be rich—children, length of days, and enduring wisdom.

What is so fascinating about understanding pain and sorrow as a divine gift is how many people throughout the generations have found comfort in this idea. In all honesty, I don't and never have. This approach has always struck me as a black-is-white or white-is-black answer, reinterpreting an evil as if it were its polar opposite. I don't believe it and I am not alone. Other Talmudic rabbis were not of one mind on this matter: "Rabi Hiyya bar Abba fell ill and Rabi Yohanan (known as a healer) went to visit him. Rabi Yohanan said to him: 'Are your sufferings welcome to you?' Rabi Hiyya bar Abba replied: 'Neither they nor their reward.'"[49] In other words, Rabi Hiyya refuses to see in his own suffering any challenge from God that ought to be accepted happily in expectation of some subsequent reward. A later passage reveals that Rabi Yohanan was as unhappy about suffering or its benefits as was his friend Rabi Hiyya bar Abba. Suffering is suffering, and as one distraught daughter

---

48   After Berakhot 5a

49   Berakhot 5b

who had watched her mother deteriorate on life support for three months blurted out to me, "This whole thing sucks!" She was right.

Another approach to the predicament, one that is hardly above criticism but one that is perhaps more realistic, is to question the extent to which God is in control. Some may regard the very question as blasphemous, as if God's unquestionable and infinite power was itself in doubt. But modern thinkers have, in fact, questioned God's limitless power. For others, God's ultimate power is not so much in question, but the extent to which God chooses to exercise that absolute power is. In either case, God is viewed as having failed to stop the evil either because of inability or unwillingness. That's a gutsy, maybe arrogant charge leveled against God. Nonetheless, the accusers, odd as it may seem, do so in defense of God.

The pragmatism of the accusation emanates from another equally important aspect of theology: free will. One may never think of free will as playing a role in theology, but it does. Here's how: If God were in charge of EVERYTHING, that means that God also controls people, our thoughts and actions. If God controls our thoughts and actions, that would also mean that this "good God" denies human beings free will. Is that something we really want to believe—either about ourselves or of God? A God who denies humans free will, like supervisors who micromanage their subordinates' every move, would strike many as neither good nor just. Moreover, if humanity has no free will, the court and our system of justice becomes a mockery, for no one can be held accountable in a world in which they are incapable of willful action. Flip Wilson (1933-1998), a popular American comedian, used to dress up as a character named Geraldine, and whenever Geraldine was caught doing something not quite kosher, or possibly completely illegal, she would defend herself claiming, "The Devil made me do it." So too, in a society where there is no recognized free will. Whatever wrong is perpetrated is never the responsibility of the perpetrator. If all action unfolds only by God's design, then in fact all crime must be attributed to God, a concept which undermines any form of jurisprudence that seeks to hold people responsible for their bad behavior.

So it is the case that to champion free will is to equally affirm a God who is loath to divine intervention, whose powers, in a word, are limited. God need not be in charge of everything in order to earn those divine bonafides as just and good. In limiting God's own powers, God grants humans freedom of action and thought, which is both kind and just. I certainly want my free will and I presume most people would as well. The alternative would be to exchange free will for automation, to become the robots of God. That sounds like a cross between a sci-fi and a Woody Allen movie. The irony here is that the fullness of our humanity lies with our ability to act freely, but our ability to act freely will also be a primary reason for an imperfect world, a place of many sorrows and sufferings. Our lives are impacted by the decisions, reasonable and unreasonable, of others. We can repeatedly wag our fingers at heaven for the perceived ills of this world, but so many of those ills are the products of human thoughtlessness and greed, stupidity and jealousy. Still, how can a good God be so indifferent to human misbehavior or uncaring about the violence committed against all known ethical standards? How can God remain so silent in the face of terrible and widespread crime?

The rabbis would argue that God is most loving and caring, which is the reason why God gave humanity the single most important gift of all time: The Torah. It is through Torah, the word of God, with all of its rules and regulations, that allows for a more loving and compassionate creation to cooperate with and respect one another. If all people were committed to the ethical word of God, the world would indeed look very different than it does today. Then again, there are those who may just argue that things are not quite as bad as they seem.

Another way of looking at the theodicy question is to actually question the question: Do the righteous in fact suffer while the evil prosper? This line of questioning may also *prima facie* sound heartless, especially given the plight of so many innocents. Nonetheless, to assert that the innocent suffer while the guilty do not presupposes as fact that which itself is unexamined. Even a rather cursory review of the facts might raise a few reservations about the assumption, owing to a multitude of evidence that the guilty are punished via fines or prison, broken lives and general unhappiness. This would stand in contrast with the innocents or righteous who ultimately do gain reward and honor for their efforts and attainments. Be that as it may, and even with offering all the evidence in the world to the contrary, the theodicy question endures. It's as if the question itself deflects any attempt at a deeper examination. Must this be the case? Is this question a sacred cow, unassailable and beyond reproach?

It has long been noted that news focuses on either the negative or the unusual. Among the negatives would be mass shootings, economic woes, traffic accidents, racism and prejudice of all forms, disease, crime, international tensions, and of course, terror and war. Among the unusual would be an Indonesian man who claims to be 146 years of age, Joey Chestnut winning the Nathan's Hot Dog Challenge by eating seventy-two hotdogs in ten minutes, or the Chicago Cubs winning the 2016 World Series, for the first time in 108 years. Ask anyone in the media business why this unique focus on the negative and the unusual and the answer will be, understandably, economics. Bad or unusual news sells. What is routine or common does not. Imagine a media outlet that reported only the ordinary. Does anyone really care to know that on Saturday, March 8, 2014, much of the country's residents arose a bit later than usual, restaurants and cinemas remained open, little leagues throughout the country played hockey and basketball, millions upon millions of people went about their lives without incident? It's not news. There's nothing new or different about it. But in fact, that day, there was other news and very unusual, alarming news at that. Malaysian Air 370, with 239 on board, took off from Kuala Lumpur International Airport, headed for Beijing, and then disappeared. It was still news the next day when the jet remained missing. It was news the following day as well, the aircraft's location still unknown. As of this writing, almost five years later, the aircraft remains missing but in a sad retreat to resignation, its missing-ness is no longer news. The next news would be if it is ever found. After a few years of mystery surrounding its whereabouts, finding the jet would be unusual. The point is that people are drawn to the unusual. And if the unusual is also negative, all the better, as researchers have found a fascination with the negative built into human DNA. John Cacioppo (1951-2018), a pioneer in the field of social neuroscience, conducted experiments in response to stimuli that would produce either positive, negative or neutral feelings. His research showed that the brain's cerebral cortex surged with electrical activity when responding to the negative stimuli, far greater than when exposed to the neutral or positive stimuli. Our attitudes, he determined, are far more influenced by the negatives than the positives, perhaps an evolutionary development that allowed humans to more accurately anticipate and recognize trouble.[50] And the more extreme the case, the greater the attention given to it. A small earthquake that creates a rumble may be of interest. But an earthquake that topples buildings and buries living beings— human and animal—that's a story that has the public reading down the full article.

---

50   Hara Estroff Marano writing in *Psychology Today,* "Our Brain's Negative Bias," June 20, 2003, https://www.psychologytoday.com/us/articles/200306/our-brains-negative-bias.

"Why do the righteous suffer while the wicked prosper?" Do they? Or does the human predilection for the outrageous, the negative, and the unusual compel us to focus more on the suffering of the righteous while discounting the good that justly falls to the deserving. Will people take greater umbrage at the suffering of the innocent than the punishment of the guilty, allowing the injustices of the world to overshadow and marginalize instances of justice?

On November 28, 1994, a man in Portage, Wisconsin, was brutally beaten to death by another man using a twenty-inch metal bar. The murderer had repeatedly smashed the man's head against a wall and after being discovered on a restroom floor where the assault had taken place, the man died about an hour later at a local hospital. This was a news item that might have garnered far more attention than it did, horrific narrative that it was, but the media gave it relatively little attention. The victim was a man by the name of Jeffrey Dahmer, a sex offender and serial killer from Milwaukee, Wisconsin, who was convicted of murdering some seventeen men and boys between 1978 and 1991. As he was a cannibal, he consumed the flesh of some of his victims. His crimes garnered widespread coverage in the media during the time of his arrest and trial. In stark contrast, his cold-blooded murder did not evince the sort of public outrage that accompanies the murder of an innocent or good person. Why? Because in the end, few beyond his own family ultimately cared about Dahmer. For some, his life in prison was immunity from what he really deserved—the death sentence. And when he was murdered by a fellow prisoner who was probably schizophrenic (he claimed God told him to commit the crime), people were not outraged by this apparent lack of prison security, or how a mentally-ill prisoner could have secured a twenty-inch metal bar, or why Dahmer and his assailant were left unsupervised. The sentiment was, more or less, that Dahmer finally got what he deserved. The wicked had been punished. That's the way the world ought to operate and that's why the story made a tiny ripple in the press, and was dropped soon thereafter.

The righteous suffer and the wicked prosper, except when they don't. The theodicy question remains a serious question and will remain so, but it is important to remember that the contours of this question have been shaped out of examples and evidence that are carefully selected by minds outraged by injustice and violence, and less exercised by justice and love. When the theodicy question does not take into account the kind and deserving people who are rewarded, any conclusions drawn will naturally be distorted. Some of the righteous do suffer, but clearly not all of them and certainly not all the time. And the wicked do prosper, but clearly not all of them and certainly not all the time.

Recalling again that the classic formulation of the theodicy question is an exaggeration for reasons of clarity, and that we are really addressing the apparent inequities of common folk who deserve better and the undeserving who benefit beyond their due, we might convincingly argue that the common folk really do come out ahead. This is really an issue of lifestyle and the choices people make. A life of crime takes people down a certain path that a law-abiding life will not. A life of boozing and carousing, drugs and gambling takes people down a certain path that a life of responsibility and conscientiousness will not. At the same time, acts of civil disobedience in the name of justice may in the end bring with it rewards that a life of apathy and social blindness will not. It's almost impossible to generalize, but it is negligent to ignore the patterns, especially as revealed in hindsight.

I once stood in the hospital with the daughter of a recently deceased woman. "I don't understand it," she said. "My mother lit candles every Shabbat, kept a kosher home, attended Shabbat services regularly, believed in God fervently. How could God have taken her like this!" She was weeping and overcome with sadness. And I, too, felt her frustration and sorrow. At the time of this heart-wrenching reproach, it was abundantly clear that she was not asking a theological question. She was testifying to the pain of theodicy itself, for theodicy is not only an academic/theological question, but it is also a painful and sorrowful reality for those in the throes of or witnessing life's challenges. After all the pious words are committed to writing, all the learned discourses spoken, all the heated exchanges concluded, sometimes the only decent response to the reality of theodicy is the warmth of a human embrace, the silence of a companion who shares in the pain, the solicitude of a community that refuses to ignore a cherished member in need. But after a few months, after the pain had subsided, the truth could be more deftly explored. It was not God who took her mother's life. It was an 18-year-old and his buddies, high on drugs and driving his Daddy's car, speeding and swerving down the Southern State. Blaming God is so much easier than confronting the teen, or his parents, or society, all of whom may just respond defensively, or unsympathetically, or possibly even angrily. In contrast, when we revile God with charges of evil, indifference, and incompetence, God absorbs it all without protest. Philosophical discussions are positively intrusive when one is deep in mourning, but after a few weeks had passed, the daughter and I were able to talk about her mother's piety and what it meant, especially in a world of free choice and free will. I knew her mother and I knew what she stood for. Her traditionalism emerged from her deep love of Judaism, connecting with God, creating family moments, reinforcing the link she had with her mother and grandparents, and supposedly the link she had hoped to create for her children and future grandchildren. Taking just one of the many rituals she observed, lighting Shabbat candles, I offered the daughter that her mother had not lit them because the ritual was designed to protect her from harm. That's superstition. She lit candles each week because Shabbat was a unique day, different from the other six, and in a world of darkness, we remember that God was the first to create light. We need more people in this world to consciously create light, in all its varied meanings, and that's what her mother hoped to do. That's what she did. And that's called faith. The next Shabbat, her daughter began lighting Shabbat candles on her own.

It's so much easier to be angry with God. One can rail against God and the imperfect justice so evident in this world and do so without fear of reprisal. That is not a dynamic available between two people, especially when they are parties to a tragedy, one the perpetrator and one the victim. Our faith in a good God is not what will protect us from the ills of the world. Our faith in a good God is what helps us navigate through the ills of the world when they strike, as they will, for they always do—the worthy and the unworthy, the deserving and the undeserving, the righteous and the wicked. No one is spared. The difference is that those with faith have tools for survival. And sometimes it takes a lifetime of practice to know how to utilize the tools when they are most desperately needed. In any event, it is always important to remember that our perception of all the evil and injustice may just be an evolutionary trick of our biological selves, which keeps us focused on the negative or the unusual as a tactic of survival. But to thank God for all the good that is in our lives, daily and repeatedly, is a check on our inborn negativity. We can never self-identify as righteous or good. But in the very least, others around us should be able to look at our actions and beliefs, and feel blessed to live in the presence of people who if not completely righteous, are in the very least deserving of such an honor.

• • • • •

TO THE GOD IS GOOD SKEPTIC

*The assumption that the righteous suffer and the wicked pros-
per may just be our biology focusing on the negative or the
unusual, a remnant of self-protective behavior from a bygone
age. Things may not be quite as bad as they seem, and when
they are, it's easier to blame God, than own up to humanity's willful disregard of the rules. There is no freedom without accountability.*

10 THE BIBLE-GOT-SEX-ALL-WRONG SKEPTIC

Do the Bible and the rabbis have anything to teach us about sexuality? And isn't the prohibition against homosexuality a reason enough for just how backwards the Bible is?

One day, Kathy came to see me about a moral issue she was struggling with and wanted my take on the situation. She was a divorced mother of one child, and she worked in the world of investment banking. She was not a regular at services, but someone who came to synagogue enough for me to know that her Judaism meant a great deal to her, and someone whose background included a respect for Torah learning. Her question revolved around dressing for business. I knew this was serious because virtually no one comes to me for fashion advice, as well they shouldn't. I shop for clothing once every four or five years, and then most of that loathsome experience unfolds in either Costco or Sears. In any event, Kathy's dilemma involved the morality of using dress to exude a sexiness that might create a material advantage for her in business. I knew exactly what she was talking about. In the predominantly male world of investment banking, she was acutely aware of how her dress might attract and then sustain a relationship—business only— which she could then turn into dollars. Kathy was an attractive woman, and knew how to dress to her advantage. But was it moral to do so? What were the ethics behind flashing a little cleavage or cutting an inch or so off the hemline to gain market share? It was an interesting question. Excluding the option of deliberately making oneself unattractive or dumpy, I suggested that modest dress need not necessarily make anyone less attractive or even compromise whatever material advantages one would otherwise have with a more revealing wardrobe. Without denying the role dress plays in sexual attraction, it probably is far less important than so often credited. People have been drawn to each other well before the advent of Versace. The rest of the story continues with Kathy's several trips to Bloomingdales, Nordstrom's, etc., none of which I can attest to. Her dilemma, however, points to a fact of social reality: sexual attraction is present in almost every human interaction, and thus the question of its healthy or unhealthy expressions is grist for moral reflection.

Sexual attraction is an ever-present force, and it is fairly independent of dress. It exists to a greater or lesser degree in all relations—between relatives, casual friends, and strangers. It exists between employees, between management and labor, and between business people and their clients. It is always there, not because humans are sneaky, perverted, or deviant beings, but because we are human, and sexuality is simply a part of our humanity. Most people learn how to mediate that sexuality within the parameters of accepted social conventions. And then, of course, some of our fellow homo sapiens do not. Judaism has always recognized the presence of the sexual dynamic as a fact of life, not a sin. In fact, it is very much regarded as a blessing, a true gift of God. Both in the Bible and later sacred literature, sexual allusions are not uncommon when describing the love of God and the people of Israel, especially within the Kabbalistic or mystical tradition. On the other hand, Jewish tradition created some well-defined boundaries within which proper sexual relations could unfold, namely by identifying those relationships that would be forbidden. Leviticus 20:10-21 lists a number of forbidden alliances, including the much-debated and widely-censured prohibition against homosexuality. But it was in the very fact of defining those forbidden relations that the Torah opens the faithful to sexual relations that would be acceptable and fulfilling.

In thinking about all the various manifestations of human sexuality, from something as simple as holding hands to wild unbridled passion, most Jews have grown up with a certain degree of latitude in exploring their sexual selves and the sexuality of their partners. Few of us grew up in the segregated culture of the *haredim*, the ultra-Orthodox Jews, where a woman might be expected to cover her hair lest she arouse the passions of someone other than her husband, or where meals might be segregated by gender, or where so much as a female and male hand clasping in a rather business-like handshake might be regarded as provocative, a sexual faus pax of sorts. As foreign as these customs may sound, they do nevertheless point to the sexual potential in almost every encounter between people. *Kol ishah ervah*—A woman's voice is sexually provocative,[51] so the rabbis say, and I don't think they were wrong. They were only remiss in not acknowledging the sexual timbre of the male voice as well. There is an observation by at least one rabbi in the Talmud that to gaze at the little finger of a woman would be akin to gazing at a far more intimate part of her body.[52] I don't think he meant to denigrate women or objectify them. And it was certainly not meant to sexualize a woman, for it seems from the rabbis' perspective that a woman needed no sexualizing. She was sexual from the start, no more and no less than men. The rabbinic focus on women has more to do with their predominately male perspective, there being no female rabbis or students in the study halls as there are today. But in the end, the rabbis' thinking would not be unlike our own: we are all sexual beings, and the sexual dynamics between us cannot be suspended indefinitely. So the question for the Jewish people was never how to quash the sexual drive, only how to channel it, to allow its expression within boundaries that a community would understand as acceptable and reasonable. The rabbis comprehended who human beings were quite well, perhaps even better than we do today, though our answers to

---

51   Berakhot 24a

52   Ibid.

what constitutes acceptable sexual expression may differ from their own.

This question has never been more relevant than it is today at a time when the sexual mores of western civilization seem so radically different than they were only a couple decades ago. The sexual revolution of the 1960's has generated a mixed legacy, creating on the one hand a freedom of sexual expression which people presumably desire, but not necessarily any enhanced commitment to long-term relationships. The effects are an increase in casual sex, where the commitment to one another may go no further than an affair conducted on the QT. The Pew Research Center reports that the number of Americans choosing to live with one another sans marriage is on the rise, with some 50% of that group aged 35 years or younger.[53] Those who distance themselves from marital bliss will certainly mingle with others. But these relationships will remain predominantly unofficial, merely casual. And it's not that a fling or an affair won't keep some people satisfied. They probably will, but only for those whose expectations of what a long-term loving relationship can be are relatively glum.

When I sit down with a couple about to be married, I record the respective addresses of the bride and groom. Thirty or twenty years ago the bride would give me her address and the groom would give me his. Today, 99% of the time, there is only one address shared by the two. I am not naïve enough

---

53   8 Facts About Love and Marriage in America, Abigail Geiger and Gretchen Livingston, http://www.pewresearch.org/fact-tank/2018/02/13/8-facts-about-love-and-marriage/

to think that shared habitation was not around in my youth or earlier. The difference is that if it was going on, you wouldn't announce it to the rabbi. Today that is no longer the case. By way of a second example, and now we turn to the other end of the lifespan continuum, we have witnessed seniors, widows and widowers, pairing up, looking after each other and caring for each other in mutually beneficial relationships. Most of the time, the community celebrates when two people who have been left alone find the companionship they so richly deserve. They take meals together, share evenings together, and take vacations together. The only thing that so many are not taking together are the sacred wedding vows that would make the relationship official. This is less a judgment than it is an observation. Nonetheless, it does lead to the following question: Is there something morally and ethically different today than years ago or have we repudiated important moral strictures that have compromised the respect and reverence we owe each other?

Some may find it surprising to learn that there is no specific ruling in the Torah prohibiting premarital sex. This is not to say that premarital sex is permitted, only that the prohibition does not have its roots in our most fundamental teaching, the Torah. Where then does it come from? It comes specifically from the rabbis. It was the rabbis who took measures to prohibit, or at least strongly discourage, premarital sex or sexual relations outside the context of marriage. There are at least three pragmatic reasons for this prohibition, none of which sound terribly godly.

The first is that the prohibition of premarital sex would serve to limit out-of-wedlock pregnancies. Forget about the *shanda* (Yiddish for shame) involved in such a phenomenon. The real issue was probably financial: Who is going to support this mother and child at a time when women have no assured source of income? Out-of-wedlock pregnancies were a financial challenge for a family and a community. Secondly, if premarital sex led to promiscuous sex, and those sexual encounters led to pregnancy, the question of paternity becomes real. Who is the father? The paternity question is again a financial question. If the father of the baby was indeterminate, ascertaining whose responsibility it is for supporting the baby and the mother is also indeterminate. In addition, any ambiguity in paternity would entail confusion over matters of inheritance, which could lead to protracted and bitter legal battles. Finally, the rabbis were not immune to Plato's distinction between the material and the spiritual worlds. Though the rabbis never dismissed the material world as thoroughly as did Plato, they did understand that mind had to prevail over matter, that the physical urge had to be tempered by a superior spiritual inclination, and thus there was a virtue in opposing one's natural drives if only in order to serve a more noble and more spiritual objective. All of this led to a prohibition of sexual expression outside the context of marriage in spite of the absence of such a prohibition in the Torah.

Leaving the Medieval period and re-entering modernity will find these concerns significantly diminished. Out-of-wedlock pregnancies may no longer be the challenge they once were. Birth control is so much more effective today than ever, and when pregnancy does occur, abortion becomes if not an ethical option, a legal and available option. Alternatively, a pregnant woman who has money in the bank or, unlike her medieval predecessor, is economically self-sufficient, may decide to see the pregnancy through, since financial concerns may be substantially muted. Thus out-of-wedlock pregnancies may no longer be a looming financial drain on a community. Some women clearly choose to have a baby without an official father involved. They may do this for a variety of reasons, but chief among them is the fact that financial self-sufficiency permits them to do so. What about the paternity issue? Today DNA testing can more or less resolve that matter. What about the control of one's lower, animalistic urges in the service of a higher more spiritual objective? It's true that people could conceivably still be motivated by that idea, but a Kinsey Institute research study entitled, "Has Virginity Lost Its Virtue? Relationship Stigma Among Sexually Inexperienced Adults" found that a majority of those polled believe that the appropriate age for the beginning of sexual relationships is between 16-19 years of age.[54] In fact, the Kinsey Institute reports that the average for "first intercourse is 16.8 for males and 17.2 years of

---

54   Has Virginity Lost Its Virtue? Kinsey Study Finds Adults Who Wait to Have Sex are Stigmatized, April 19, 2016, https://viewpoints.iu.edu/health-and-vitality/2016/04/19/has-virginity-lost-its-virtue-kinsey-study-finds-adults-who-wait-to-have-sex-are-stigmatized/

age for females.[55] The rabbis would not be surprised with the findings of the Kinsey Institute.

In Pirkei Avot, the predetermined agenda for a Jewish man's life is outlined. "At five he studies Bible, at ten he studies Mishnah, at thirteen he becomes Bar Mitzvah, at fifteen he studies Talmud, at eighteen he stands at the *huppah*..."[56] At eighteen years of age, the young man is expected to marry and there is every reason to believe that his bride was younger than he, perhaps seventeen, sixteen, fifteen years of age or younger. That was the sociological reality of the Talmudic era. What would surprise the rabbis with the Kinsey Institute's findings is the fact that these young people were not married. They would not be disturbed with the reality of sexual relationship at so young an age, but would bristle with the idea that such activity is acceptable between two people who were not in some way materially committed to one another.

Halakhah or the Jewish path in life was never meant to be detached from sociological reality. Of course, the greater part of Halakhah remains intact from one generation to the next, but each generation also gives it its own spin. What the rabbis regarded as the proper time for young people to marry and to thus be fully active sexually would be regarded by us as an age when kids ought to be focused on their studies. The Medieval rabbis' sociological reality and ours are two very different animals. Imagine what the congregation would think if

---

55   Kinsey Institute, https://kinseyinstitute.org/research/faq.php

56   Pirkei Avot 5:25

a rabbi were to announce over the High Holidays, "Our sons should marry at eighteen and our daughters at seventeen, sixteen, or fifteen." My assumption is that the message would be received poorly. In 2017, the median age for a first-time marriage among American males was 29.5 and for American women, 27.4.[57] That's more than eleven years later than what the rabbis had in mind. And remember, in speaking of a median, there are as many people getting married older than that as there are younger than 29.5 or 27.4 years of age. Is it reasonable to expect close to half of our young people to abstain sexually, a decade or longer, beyond their having achieved sexual readiness? Is it humane?

From the very beginning of the Torah, we learn "it is not good for a person to be alone."[58] There is a basic need for human companionship that seems hard-wired into our constitution and consciousness. That need is addressed when two people are able to find each other and establish a relationship based on a mutual recognition of each other's dignity, self-worth, and humanity. We can be fairly certain that the sexual expressions emanating from a relationship of that temperament will be healthy and moral. There is most likely a spiritual dimension to a sexual relationship of that nature, whether recognized or not.

Oscar Wilde (1854-1900), the Irish poet and playwright, is purported to have said, "Everything in the world is about sex, except sex. Sex is about power." If thought were food, we

---

57   Women's Health, *This is the Average Age for Marriage Right Now,* Marcaela Mackenzie, https://www.womenshealthmag.com/relationships/a19567270/average-age-of-marriage/

58   Genesis 2:18

could chew on this one for a decade. Everything is about sex? Sex is about power? Much has been written about Wilde's perception, but few have dismissed it. And the reason is that even if the saying is not immediately intelligible, it's a thought that catches one off-guard and compels each of us to think—why do I do what I do sexually, and who am I when I yearn for sex?

Let's begin with the obvious. Sexual expression does not always transpire within a loving, mutually-respectful relationship. This is true because, as Wilde points out, sex is about power—not always, but sometimes it is. Non-consensual sex is not an act of love; it is an assault. It is about domination of a superior over a subordinate. Rape is a form of sexual violence, totally devoid of any spiritual dimension. By the same token, a sexuality that is characterized by a deliberate domination of one partner over the other is not necessarily of questionable morality. Its moral status would hinge on whether the relationship was consensual and welcomed or not. "Who am I when I yearn for sex?" is a critical question about the nature of our own character and motivation. Is our sexual yearning a desire for a forced domination over another? Within the context of a specific relationship, is domination and submission consensual or not? In a heterosexual context, might sexuality be the domination of a man over a woman, as if a man were conquering a woman? To put it in another way, is sexuality a relationship between two unequal partners, where the one with greater power dominates the weaker? Many may be horrified to think of sexuality in these terms, but history proves time and time

again that the domination/submission motif in human relationships was more common than presently acknowledged. In
ancient Greece and Rome, older men established relations with
younger boys. The power differential was very clear and surprisingly, socially acceptable.

In recent times, the #MeToo phenomenon has brought to
light the extent to which power differential has played an inglo-
rious role among people who were leaders in their respective
professions. Though almost all of these sexual assaults were
perpetrated by men against women, it became abundantly
clear and public that the assault had to do with one person with
much power versus another with less. It was a movie mogul
versus a young actress, a TV anchor versus an employee, a successful entrepreneur versus an unsuspecting associate. Sadly,
many of these accusations crescendoed into a conviction tried
in the court of public opinion, the least reliable court in the
entire world. And it's very possible that some accusations were
exaggerated in unfair and unjust ways. But as Matt Lauer, the
popular co-host of NBC's Today Show for some twenty years,
said after he was fired over such accusations, some of which
he described as exaggerated, "there is enough truth in these
stories to make me feel embarrassed or ashamed."

Sexuality as aggression is openly acknowledged in one
of the most common and vulgar of all imprecations: F**k You!
How odd a curse! Is intercourse meant to be pleasure or punishment? Why would one person in a relationship, frustrated

or impatient, angry or hateful, turn to the other and tell that person to do something pleasurable?

"I hate your guts—Go get a chocolate mint ice cream!"

"You're the most miserable person on the face of the earth—Take a day off and relax!"

The curse we are so familiar with makes no sense unless sexuality can be understood, under given circumstances, as an act of aggression, as an unequal relationship in which the powerful dominates, and in the case of the curse, assaults the weaker. Within the sexual culture of ancient Greece, partners were less identified by gender as they were by the active versus the passive player, the penetrator versus the penetrated. And in that sexual culture, the penetrator corresponded to higher social status, adulthood, and masculinity, whereas the penetrated corresponded to lower social status, femininity, and youth. The Greeks left a large library's worth of graphic depictions in sculpture and pottery of unequal, homosexual behavior. The same was also true of Roman society where older men consorted with boys in accepted sexual unions. But even in a social structure regarded abhorrent by contemporary standards, Rome had its "sacred" boundaries. The Roman Emperor Elagabalus (218-222 CE) was regarded as a particularly immoral and decadent individual. He married five times, sired no children, perhaps owing to his homosexuality. The Romans were not upset with his having male lovers, of which he had many, as did so many of the Roman elite. Rather, they were upset that he played the submissive role in the homosexual encounter, thus playing the penetrated rather than the penetrator. This was antithetical to the emperorship, for the emperor must always be dominant.

The ancient Israelites rejected these sexual practices, idealizing and sanctifying only love between a man and a woman. They must have understood the unequal power dynamics in sexuality, though in their very patriarchal society, such domination could be moral only when expressed conventionally as that of a man over a woman. This is the hidden underpinning of the Torah's prohibition against homosexuality, but not lesbianism. Homosexuality is prohibited in the Torah because it would apply to a man treating another man as if he were a woman, one man dominating another. Such domination would be intolerable in a society that sought to equalize all men as having been created in the image of God.[59] On the other hand, few in a patriarchal society would necessarily care about a woman dominating another woman, as women were viewed as subordinate to begin with. It would be a man's domination of another man that would be read as a sociological trespass deserving of censure. Such an understanding of homosexuality would make the language of the Torah's prohibition perfectly understandable: "Do not lie with a male as one lies with a woman: it is an abomination."[60] If this is the reason behind the prohibition of homosexuality, then such a prohibition begins to dissipate in

---

59   Genesis 1:27

60   Leviticus 18:22

a world where the ideal sexual relationship has nothing to do with domination, but mutuality.

The reigning public discourse about physical intimacy is focused on sexual safety, a very important message to be sure, but equally important would be a message regarding sexual integrity. With sex having been stripped of even the pretense of marriage, sex can now be addressed independent of any long-term commitment. In our anxiety and apprehension about the spread of sexually transmitted diseases, we strip sexuality of context and simply talk about the pill or condoms. We talk about sexuality precisely the way the rabbis feared it could be reduced to if torn from the context of a loving, faithful, mutually-respectful relationship. The most prominent public caveat to the sexually-active today is this: do it safely. There is no question that this is a biologically-worthy message, but the insatiable human appetite for meaning forever brings us back to one gnawing reality: we are all more than our biology.

At a time when teens are struggling with their own identities and of questions about adulthood and morality, it's very difficult for them to fully appreciate someone else. This is not to say that we should expect teenagers to be divorced from sexual behavior. To the contrary, their experimentation and exploration with each other helps them grow and mature. But rather than impose on them some artificial segregation by gender, we need to give them clear and reasonable boundaries, and above all, a sexuality that lives within the context of a serious relationship. The same holds true for anyone longing for human companionship. What kind of a relationship do they seek? What do they long for most? Is their desire to establish a mutually, loving relationship? Is their desire only for a transitory encounter? Is that fair or moral with a partner expecting something more? Is that fair or moral with a partner expecting no more than that?

The ultimate spiritual relationship would be one that transpires within the context of *kiddushin,* sanctity, which is precisely the name for marriage in rabbinic jargon. It's almost impossible for teenagers to achieve the spiritual state that *kiddushin* implies, given their youth, and the work they need to do in order to discover themselves. In the end, what will determine the moral or spiritual dimension of a given sexual encounter, will not be a rule whether premarital sex is permitted or not, but it will be whether two people can establish a mutually-respectful and mutually-loving relationship or not. Freedom may permit people to be promiscuous, and science and technology have freed both men and women in ways that prior generations could never dream, but our tradition will not recognize any spiritual dimension, any moral legitimacy to the casual encounters of the one-night stand, or the desire to maintain multiple partners, or the decision to pay for play. When the other person is used as a means to satisfy a sexual need, it is not the sexuality that we have debased, it is rather the person herself or himself. And in a world-view that would demand "love your fellow as yourself"[61] that is unacceptable.

----

61   Leviticus 19:18

The problem with *kiddushin* is that at the heart of the ceremony, and at the foundation of the marital status which it establishes, is an acquisition of one person by another. In a traditionally Orthodox ceremony, the point at which the groom gives the bride a ring, he recites as follows: "By this ring, you are *mekudeshet* (consecrated) to me, in accordance with the laws of Moses and the people of Israel." In this way, the groom essentially acquires the bride, and as such, establishes a relationship which is de jure unequal. Do moderns in the twenty-first century really embrace the idea of marriage as acquisition or of one taking possession of another? Do even modern Orthodox Jews believe it? Most likely not. This is an example of a tradition that has persisted beyond the belief system that created it.

There are ways to mitigate the inequality of the ceremony. So for example, instead of there being only one exchange of rings, from groom to bride, there can be a second exchange, from bride to groom. Instead of there being only one declaration recited by the groom, there can be a second one declared by the bride. Nonetheless, the fact that *kiddushin* is an act of acquisition is beyond dispute, and given the thrust of how Jewish tradition has seen fit to reject superior/subordinate relationships, particularly in its historical opposition to homosexuality, one must necessarily question if the same should not be true in a heterosexual relationship. Some may resist the answer in their devotion to tradition, but few would dispute the predominant social value that human beings are independent and free and no one is permitted to own another.

I have, as of late, created a modified *kiddushin,* in which the bride and groom exchange rings simultaneously, and recite simultaneously (in Hebrew) the following: "By these rings, we are *mekudashim hadadi* (mutually consecrated) to each other in accordance with the laws of Moses and the people of Israel." I do this because ultimately, a contemporary Judaism cannot justify ownership of one human being by another, and can only promote a de jure mutually respectful and appreciative relationship between two equal partners. And that goes for homosexual couples as it would for heterosexual couples. The greatest irony here is that it is the prohibition on homosexuality in the context of its practice in the ancient world which sheds light on how we ought to view and promote all intimate relationships today.

The task of Judaism is to help us distinguish between the animal sexuality hardwired within us, which we can give expression to thoughtlessly, and the spiritual sexuality that we also carry within us, that diminishes our loneliness, eases our anxieties, excites us internally for who we are and for whom we recognize our partners to be. We have barely touched the surface of so many aspects of human sexuality and its various manifestations. But what we have determined is that human sexuality, far from being a sin, is a blessing, given the right context and motivations. It is a creative act, physically and emotionally. It is no wonder that intimacy on Shabbat is regarded as a double mitzvah.

• • • • •

TO THE BIBLE-GOT-SEX-ALL-WRONG SKEPTIC

Judaism instructs us to use our sexuality in a mutually respectful way, ideally within the context of a long term loving and monogamous relationship. We thus elevate sexuality beyond biology into the realm of the spiritual, where the truly satisfying relationships reside.

11 THE IN-MARRIAGE SKEPTIC

*This tradition just ends up insulting Jews
and non-Jews alike. Plus, it's racist.
What's the point?*

Heather was raised in an observant Jewish family that belonged to my synagogue. She was deeply involved with the congregation's youth groups, enjoyed socializing, and went off to college with hopes of securing a bachelor's degree and perhaps an available Jewish bachelor as well. During her years at college, she met with me on several occasions to discuss her social life. There were plenty of Jewish boys at the university she attended and she was close on a couple of occasions to settling into a long-term relationship, but in the end, something always got in the way. It was her religious observance. She liked to go to services on Shabbat—not every Shabbat, but periodically. She spoke about belonging to a synagogue someday. She kept kosher, not of the "I can't eat in a non-kosher restaurant" variety, but she was careful with what she ordered when dining out. Her observance was a turn-off for the boys she dated.

The tears would slowly make their way down her cheeks when reflecting on her frustrations.

Years later, now in her early thirties, Heather told me she was engaged. "Mazal Tov," I said, to which she replied, "But he's not Jewish." I was a bit surprised, a surprise she had anticipated, and she went on to explain. "Rabbi—he's the first guy I've ever dated who hasn't made fun of my keeping kosher." She wasn't looking for my sympathy; she was truthfully telling me her experience, and from a purely liberal Jewish sociological perspective, it was a deeply sad tale. To make matters worse, I was about to make matters worse. She asked if I would officiate at her wedding, and I responded, as do all rabbis of the Rabbinical Assembly, the international professional organization of Conservative rabbis, "I'm so sorry, but no, I cannot."

Heather was a real person with whom I had a very positive relationship. She was unique. After college she worked as an accountant in a major Manhattan firm, living on her own terms with the intent of marrying a Jewish man. Many of her contemporaries, and I dare say an increasing number of young Jewish people today, do not share her proclivities. To the contrary, they leave home to mix and socialize with many different people of varied ethnic, religious, and racial backgrounds where they are accepted as equals. And these young people are, within the context of the American Jewish experience, what we would call success stories.

What makes them success stories are the ways in which they have so thoroughly integrated into their personal lives the values that predominate the liberal world of Western democracies, values that the liberal Jewish world have embraced and promoted to varying degrees. These values include a respect for all people regardless of their ethnic, religious, or racial background; a distancing if not a total rejection of any notion that Jewishness is a superior tradition or that Jews are in some way chosen; and a suspicion that seriously religious people are in some way simple-minded or foolish. These values are the very values that predominate the universities that young Jewish people compete to enter. Rabbi Jeffrey K. Salkin wrote about an incident in his freshman year at college when the subject of religion was at issue in a Psychology class. Salkin had just admitted to being a committed Jew and one with a belief in God. The professor's response was one of dismay and he consequently expressed the hope that the young Salkin would, with time, begin to question that faith. The episode was forgotten to Salkin until recently when a Pew study found more than half of Jews who had not completed college to believe in God with absolute certainly, as compared with only 30% of Jewish college graduates admitting to that same solid belief. The study also determined that 39% of all Jews who had not completed college said that religion was very important in their lives, as compared with only 25% of Jewish college graduates.[62]

In addition to the highly secularized messages transmitted to young Jewish people, there is one other very non-Western message that parents and rabbis sometimes throw into the

---

62   Rabbi Jeffrey K. Salkin, "Are Smart Jews Too Cool for Shul?" http://religionnews.com/2017/04/28/jews-pew-education-religious/ April 28, 2017

mixture: "Non-Jews are fine, but don't marry one." It's a message that for all intents and purposes, given all the other messages, is a glorious non-sequitur. It simply doesn't follow. How can one embrace a philosophical diet of "all people are equal; respect everyone regardless of background; do not regard yourself as superior; don't get too religious...and 'DON'T MARRY A NON-JEW'"? At another period in Jewish history, when Jews may have regarded themselves as chosen and their Judaism as superior to other traditions, the "Don't marry a non-Jew" message followed logically. But the liberal Jewish world has changed the way it views itself and others, and suddenly, the message of endogamy, that is of marrying within the group, is a weighty message hanging by diminishing threads of justification. Given all this, has the time come for Jews to acknowledge their altered perspective of themselves and the world, abandon the tradition of endogamy, and accept the reality of interfaith marriages? Has the time come for someone like me to accommodate someone like Heather?

This question is hardly a new one. It seems as if it has been hotly debated for at least half a century, if not longer. And having dealt with the matter periodically over the years, I can honestly attest to an issue that raises the passions and emotions of the Jewish people, whether one is for or against. In 2000, an American Jewish Committee survey found that 50% of Jews interviewed thought it racist to oppose Jewish-gentile marriages.[63] That left 47% of those polled believing it was not.

---

63   The New York Times, *Marriage Issue Splits Jews, Poll Finds*, Gustav Niebuhr, October 31, 2000

That's about as divided as a community can get. Any rabbi thrown into that divide is either going to disappoint one half of the congregation or the other, or will choose to not address the topic directly, thus keeping everyone in suspense. On occasion, this is not a terrible tactic. As diplomatic as sitting on a fence may be, it's time to get off, and the question is, on which side should rabbis disembark.

The fence metaphor is here by design, as it should be clear that the issue at hand is one of where to draw the line. And this, in and of itself, is a very interesting question because we are presently caught in a world in which lines themselves are under attack. The sentiment here seems to be that there is something ghastly about the lines drawn in the world, even those imposed by nature, or perhaps it should be said—especially those imposed by nature. For example, most of the world grows up thinking that there are essentially two genders, male and female, and that these genders are based on unique anatomies which are typically easily identifiable. In contrast, contemporary gender studies would have us believe that gender is a social construct separate and apart from one's biology. That is to say, a person who is biologically a man may think of himself as a woman, in which case, he is really a she. Or the opposite, a person who is biologically a woman may think of herself as a he, in which case she is really a he. This is not to say that such people are lying or engaged in a grandiose hoax, but it is a radical departure from how thousands of generations of humankind have identified male and female. The academic world, the world of so many liberal universities, is lobbying for such identifications to be based on personal choice. Silly as this may sound, the boundary issue here has practical ramifications in how we determine who is permitted in the men's bathroom or the women's bathroom. And for those whose gender identification remains ambiguous, there is a movement afoot for public institutions to offer a third alternative, a restroom for the gender neutral. The point of this observation is not to be critical of those who are engaged in gender reassessments, but only to offer an example of how boundaries that were once solidly understood are now either questioned or done away with altogether.

This resistance to nature's boundaries manifests itself in serious and expensive surgeries to physically alter one's genital anatomy, or in the far more innocuous act of dying the hair in completely unnatural colors or in physical piercings that distort the shape of the body. Such alterations seem to becoming increasingly commonplace. In one particularly egregious example of how natural boundaries are challenged, a president of the National Association for the Advancement of Colored People (NAACP) was forced to resign after it was discovered that this heretofore black female president was actually born white. Rachel Dolezal has since stated that racial fluidity is just like transgenderism—race is how a person chooses to identify oneself regardless of biology. Apparently, the NAACP leadership didn't buy it. In their view, race is biological, not philosophical.

It is no wonder that one of the hottest items on the political agenda these days is the security of national borders. This is not an issue debated solely by Americans. The wars and conflicts around the world that have ignited an explosion of refugees fleeing for their lives has forced otherwise liberal countries to question the purpose of its own borders. Is there a border in place that allows for the controlled entry of foreigners or not? Should that boundary be as thick as the armor on a tank or as fluid as the curtains on one's windows? Are borders necessary or not? This discomfort with boundaries is not only writ into the social consciousness of good people who want to help the world, but has occupied a place in the very titles of organizations like Doctors Without Borders, Engineers Without Borders, Teachers Without Borders, etc.

The liberal Jewish world has also struggled with the issue of borders or boundaries, most notably that border between Jew and non-Jew. For example, many synagogues have had to debate the merits of allowing a non-Jew onto the *bimah*. There was never a question of allowing a non-Jew into the synagogue. The synagogue was never a Mecca, forbidden to all but Moslems themselves. But the *bimah* somehow seemed different and until this day, there are synagogues that do not permit non-Jews onto the *bimah* while others do.

The ramifications of boundary-ambivalence should not be underestimated for the Jewish community, as Jewish communal life for years has been based on sacred, and in most cases inviolable, boundaries. At the conclusion of Shabbat, the last blessing in *Havdalah*, the ceremony of bringing Shabbat to an end, reads as follows:

> Praised are You, Lord our God, who leads us through this amazing universe, who distinguishes between the sacred and the profane, between light and darkness, between Israel and the nations, between the Seventh Day and the six days of creation. Praised are You, Lord, for having distinguished between the sacred and the profane.

Actually, the term for sacred in Hebrew is *kadosh*, which carries with it the sense of being separate or apart. This understanding of the term flows naturally from an inventory of those items or concepts listed in the Torah as *kadosh*. So, for example, the ancient Temple in Jerusalem is *kadosh* because it is the exclusive home of God; offerings to the Temple are *kadosh* because once so designated, they cannot be used for anything other than what the priests do with them; Shabbat is *kadosh* because it is a day during which we create a unique environment, *sui generis* as compared with all the other days of the week; and additionally, the Jewish people are *kadosh*, because as the chosen ones of God, they are to act in a way that is different from all the other nations, presumably in a way that distinguishes them as completely moral in their decisions and mindful of the godliness with which the world is imbued. As Rabbi Martin S. Cohen, a prolific author and the spiritual leader of Shelter Rock Jewish Center in Roslyn, NY, once put it, "The

essence of Jewishness is the quest for *kedushah* (i.e., holiness)."
In other words, the Jew lives to create holiness, and that is done
by observing and maintaining the boundaries that elevate and
spiritualize life over and above that which would otherwise be
regarded as mundane or profane, vulgar or meaningless.

One of the most disheartening metaphors for traditional
Jews is the one that defines America as a melting pot. This metaphor is, on the one hand, a loving image of a place where people of diverse backgrounds come together and become one.
But the function of the melting pot is to dissipate boundaries,
erase distinct identities, and for a traditional community whose
understanding of sanctity is the guarding of such boundaries,
the metaphor itself is an attack on Jewish self-definition.

Then again, this problem was true only for the Jews who
held fast to traditionalism. As for the tens of thousands of Jews
who immigrated to America in the late 19th and early 20th centuries, they were only too eager to blend into America, and
do whatever necessary to achieve that objective. Those rituals that may have distinguished Jews from the community at
large—resting on Shabbat, maintaining the dietary laws, daily
prayer, clothing codes and so forth—were increasingly abandoned in favor of an assimilation that made Jews look and
behave like all the other Americans. And as Jews became
increasingly assimilated, they were also increasingly welcomed
into clubs and institutions that in an earlier era were restricted
to them. For a people locked out of the mainstream for so long,
every opened door was like manna from Heaven. The melting

pot was steaming; the boundaries were finally evaporating. In the last few decades of the twentieth century, it was becoming abundantly clear that not only were Jews and non-Jews socializing together, but they were marrying one another. The most guarded and sacred boundary of all, that boundary between Jews and everyone else, was melting away. And ever since then, this new and disruptive reality inspired a communal debate that continues to rage: Do we accept the new reality and abandon a boundary that is so widely ignored, or do we embrace the boundary even against what seems to be all odds? There should be no mistake about the broader message to the Jewish community when rabbis do agree to officiate at interfaith marriages. The broader message is that the boundary no longer exists. A community that purportedly values in-marriage while its leadership officially sanctions interfaith marriage suffers from a paradox that it ultimately cannot sustain.

If a Judaism for a contemporary world is to be at all appealing, it must first and foremost be honest. It is therefore important to begin with an admission that a message which conceives of all people as equal, worthy, and precious in the eyes of God regardless of ethnicity, religion or race, coupled with the caveat "Please don't marry them," sounds contradictory. This is the reason why many Reform, Reconstructionist, and independent rabbis willingly officiate at interfaith marriages. Conservative rabbis tend to be struggling with the merits and demerits of the practice. As for Orthodox rabbis, there seems to be little in the way of debate about the matter. There are compelling reasons on both sides of this debate. The more traditional rabbis actually do understand the sense of racism that opposition to interfaith marriage provokes. When so many of the boundaries between Jews and non-Jews have been dismantled, what remains is some vague notion of gentiles being in some way deficient, inferior, or unworthy. And that is racist. So if in-marriage is to remain a sacred Jewish value, and if the Jewish community continues to view all God's children as equal, what exactly would the rationale be for promoting in-marriage, Jew marrying Jew alone?

Membership in Jewish peoplehood requires very little. But Jewish peoplehood is only one aspect of Jewishness. There is a spiritual dimension to Jewishness that exists and is real. Some Jews embrace it fully, others reject it in toto, but most Jews are somewhere in between. That dimension of Jewish spirituality, summarized in twenty-five words or less, would run something like this:

> Jews partner with God. God will be our ultimate source of hope and inspiration and we will be God's emissaries on earth, promoting and defending all that is moral, just, and sacred.

That statement is a tad over twenty-five words, but no matter, the partnership demands flexibility and compassion so the definition stands. Because this covenant between the Jewish people and God passes from generation to generation, some people are born into it. Jews by birth may reject it all at some point. It is after all a free world. But the idea here is that Jews are born into a spiritual chain that began with Abraham and continues on to this day. That's a powerful spiritual heritage. Jewish children, the day of their birth, are already 3500 years old and welcomed into that 3500-year-old covenant.

The succession of Jewishness through the generations is not, however, based on genetics alone. And this is clear because conversion into Judaism is possible, and in many cases, welcomed. Anyone may choose to enter Jewish peoplehood via protocols that have existed for centuries. And when people choose to do so, it is reason for celebration. When people choose not to, they too deserve our respect. Judaism is a profound and inspirational path to God, but only one of many. And for some, finding a relationship with God may not be an issue at all. Nonetheless, the Jewish wedding ceremony and the marriage itself is a celebration of this age-old covenant, as it is a formal recognition of yet one more unit of Jewish loyalty that God and Jews have a deal and are committed to preserving that deal forever.

The Jewish wedding ceremony is known in Hebrew by the word *kiddushin*. *Kiddushin* shares a root with the word *kadosh* (holiness) and as such, carries with it implications of separateness and apartness. When a couple enters *kiddushin*, the two are establishing a relationship that is unique. They are vowing to be faithful to one another, that is, to establish a relationship that is exclusive, separate, and therefore special. By the same token, they are vowing to establish a relationship that is exclusive in another way. The *kiddushin* blessing begins with a formula familiar to all Jews: "...*asher kid'shanu b'mitzvotav v'tzivanu*—[God], You have distinguished us via Your mitzvot and have directed us to..." This blessing applies to Jews, but not to others. The blessing acknowledges Jews as an official party to a sacred covenant, to the partnership that commits us to a special kind of life. There is a boundary in that blessing as clear as the boundary established when the bride circles seven times around the groom.

The fifth blessing of the *Sheva Berakhot*, the traditional seven blessings of the Jewish wedding ceremony, reads as follows: "May Israel, once bereft of her children, now delight as they gather together in joy. Praised are You, God, who lets Zion rejoice with her children." One might legitimately ask why it is necessary to drag Zion into the Jewish wedding ceremony. What does Zion have to do with two young people choosing to marry? The answer lies again in *kiddushin*, this idea that the marriage begins as a call to the couple to shape their lives and their relationship in line with 3500 years of Jewish tradition, values, and continuity. It is a blessing that is designed for Jews, and only for Jews.

Now many Jews may no longer feel the call to Zion, to a God that is in covenant with Jews, to a morality that emanates from Torah, or to a narrative that stretches back so many centuries. And it should come as no surprise that there have been plenty of Jewish couples who have chosen a Justice of the Peace or a mayor of a town, or a respected friend to officiate at

their wedding precisely because they no longer want to identify with values that for them have become provincial or passé.
We do not live in a world favorably disposed to serious religious belief. But the point is this: The Jewish wedding creates a
partnership of two people who are committed to the covenant,
either by virtue of birth or by virtue of choice. When the family unit no longer needs to be bound by the covenant, when
that boundary dissipates, the spiritual dimension of Judaism
takes a serious hit, and may just be a hit from which it cannot
recover. When rabbis grant their seal of approval to marriages
in which covenant no longer figures, they are undermining the
very Judaism they are supposed to promote.

Clearly, it wouldn't be the first time that Jews in leadership chose to so alter Judaism as to make it more palatable to
a larger audience. Jewish leadership did this some 2000 years
ago. At that time, the argument was that more people would
choose Judaism if the barriers to entry weren't so high. If we
didn't require *brit milah*, or *kashrut*, or Sabbath observance,
so many more people whose choose to be Jews. These efforts
evolved into something enormously successful, the culmina-
tion of which we are very familiar with today: Christianity. But
Christianity, for all its glory and magnificence, and for the serious religious tradition that it is, is no longer Judaism.

Some time ago, a man approached me to unburden himself of an issue that had bothered him for years. He had been
married twice. His first marriage ended in divorce, a bitterly
contested and ugly divorce, but in the very least a separation

that ended fifteen years of misery. That was his Jewish marriage. His second marriage, to an Italian Catholic, was a loving, mutually respectful, and beautiful marriage. This man was, for all intents and purposes, a devoted Jew, a member of the congregation, a man who could lead prayer if so asked, and one who was forever stymied with the fact that his marriage to the "right woman" could have ended so badly while his marriage to the "wrong woman" could be so loving and fulfilling. How was he to reconcile that?

It should have been obvious, but it simply wasn't to him or to most Jews, that the issue of in-marriage deals with a Jewish communal existential issue. Can a Jew and non-Jew share a very loving and mutually respectful relationship together? Absolutely! And when that happens, it's a blessing of a deeply personal nature. But that is not the issue. The issue of in-marriage is about communal viability and continuity. Even when children are to be raised as Jews, the integration with family of other religious backgrounds, celebrating with them non-Jewish rituals, an erasure of the boundaries, as it were, creates too great a potential for a child to entertain another way of religious life. In truth, there are far worse things in the world than a Jew converting to another religious tradition. Jews sometimes underestimate the appeal of Christianity, especially in a culture where it is the dominant religion. But the interests of Jewish leadership and community must be in keeping Jews within the fold, not endorsing conditions for making it easier to leave. To look a blind eye at that potential is communal suicide.

It's not easy to say no. Ask any parent of the twenty-first century and they will admit that 'no' is the hardest word to speak. And that, too, is an affliction which emanates from the erosion of boundaries. It's an affliction which manifests itself in unacceptable dress, inappropriate language, and disrespect for figures of authority—teachers, police, clergy, and even political figures. The word 'yes' does not identify a boundary, but 'no' does. Rabbis, too, suffer from this affliction. They love to say yes and hate to say no. But rabbis have an obligation to preserve long-standing traditions, and when it comes to interfaith marriage, it is the no of today that will best preserve the Judaism of tomorrow.

· · · · ·

TO THE In-Marriage Skeptic

Guarding the boundary against interfaith marriage is not racist for a people who happily welcome converts into the community. It is, rather, a tradition that seeks to maintain the sanctity of covenant to which all Jews belong. This tradition will never be easy to maintain in a world that embraces liberal values, as Jews do, but to resolve the tension by abandoning endogamy may cause irreparable damage to the future of Jewish peoplehood.

12 THE ZIONISM SKEPTIC

Until Israel starts treating Palestinians as they should, I will have nothing to do with Israel.

In May 1948, the Zionist leaders who were about to become the political heads of a Jewish autonomous state for the first time in almost 1900 years had a problem—what was the new nation to be named? It certainly was not going to be Palestine, the name used under the British Mandate. It was the Roman Emperor Hadrian (76-138 CE) who officially named the area "Syria Palestina," this after a bloody revolt, the Bar Kochba Rebellion of 132-135 CE. The new name was meant to cut off any connection between the Jews and the land, hitherto known as Judea. The Zionists considered reverting back to the name Judea, thus winning a posthumous victory over the Romans, but owing to the fact that the contours of the new state would not include much if any of the ancient Judean boundaries, it didn't seem right. As one might expect with any Jewish vote, there were several proposals on the table. Theodore Herzl (1860-1904), the Austro-Hungarian journalist and political activist, the founder of modern political Zionism, had always referred to his proposed new state, as *Der Judenstadt* or the Jewish State. This is essentially the same term that David Ben-Gurion (1886-1973), the first prime minister of Israel, used in his pre-statehood Hebrew speeches when he spoke of *Medinat HaYehudim*—the State of the Jews. Another suggestion was *Tzabar*, after the prickly cactus by which Jews born in Palestine were called, thus comparing them with the plant that was tough on the outside, yet soft on the inside. Few liked that idea. Finally, Israel was suggested, a vote was taken and the name Israel won, 7 to 3. Years later, Ben-Gurion was interviewed about that meeting and asked whose suggestion it was to rename the new state Israel, but he couldn't remember.

The name Israel is first found in the biblical literature in the book of Genesis. The name begins with the patriarch Jacob who in an attempt to deceptively secure the blessing owed the firstborn tricks his father and robs his older brother of his rightful birthright blessing. Jacob is not alone in the ruse. It is his mother, Rebecca, who has devised the scheme as she believes her younger baby far more deserving of the blessing than her firstborn, Jacob's brother Esau. She prepares a sumptuous meal for her husband Isaac, dresses Jacob in Esau's finest clothing, and then covers his arms and neck in the furry skins of the animals just slaughtered. Blind Isaac would thus be unable to distinguish between his smooth-skinned Jacob and his hairy son Esau. The trick works, despite Isaac's suspicions, who verbalizes his doubts: "The voice is the voice of Jacob, but the hands are the hands of Esau."[64] The scheme allowed Jacob to win the battle, but sadly lose the war. Jacob did secure the firstborn blessing, but his brother's anger was extreme, and there was talk of fratricide. Jacob is forced to flee his home, his parents, all that he knew and loved, and live in exile for some twenty-two years.

A lot can happen in twenty-two years, and so it was in Jacob and Esau's lives. They both married, became exceedingly rich, and commanded the attention of many servants. When life with Jacob's unscrupulous father-in-law became unbearable, he knew the time had come to return home, but the trip back was beset with anxieties and fears. Would Esau make good on his vow to kill his little brother? Would Esau strip Jacob of his property—cattle, flocks, and servants? Would this trip home be an exercise in foolishness, an obvious walk into the throes of tragedy? Jacob obsessed over these questions. He knew he must somehow do penance for his trickery, but would any gesture of reconciliation be enough?

> Jacob was left alone, and a man wrestled with him until the break of dawn. When the man saw that he did not prevail against Jacob, he wrenched Jacob's hip at its socket, so that the socket of his hip was strained as he wrestled with him. Then he said, "Let me go, for day is breaking." But Jacob answered, "I will not let you go, unless you bless me." Said the other, "What is your name?" And he

---

64   Genesis 27:22

replied, "Jacob." Then he said, "Your name shall no longer be Jacob, but Israel, for you have striven with God and men, and have prevailed."[65]

This episode as recorded is among the most majestic in the biblical literature. It transforms Jacob, by now a very successful shepherd and businessman, into something akin to a Greek hero, for who but such a storied champion wrestles with "beings divine and human" and prevails! And on top of this, the passage is the first mention of the name Israel in the Bible. If Jacob could wrestle with God and prevail, Jacob could meet anyone, even his murderous brother, and prevail. The rest is history, or mythology, or a bit of both. Jacob did meet Esau and the two fell on each other in a loving embrace.

Jacob's family became known as *B'nei Yisra'el,* the Children of Israel. The Children of Israel occupied a specific territory in the Mediterranean, a single kingdom which later split into two, the Southern known as Judea and the Northern known as Israel. Both these kingdoms had beginnings and endings during which they flourished. With their demise, some of their citizens assimilated into the general population while others remained distinctively "Judean." Some remained in their ancestral home while others wandered. And however it was that that these Judeans ultimately became "Jews," they forever remained connected to *Eretz Yisra'el* or the Land of Israel, as testified by the *siddur,* which references return to the land

---

65   Genesis 32:25-29

repeatedly. Even in the Grace After Meals, a prayer that theoretically should require no mention of national restoration, there is mention of national restoration: "O Merciful One, break the yoke that rests on our necks and lead us directly back to our land." It's a bit incongruous to throw this into a prayer following a pastrami sandwich, but a very powerful indication of just how deep the Jewish connection with *Eretz Yisra'el* runs, and how prevalent expressions of return to her became.

How the Jewish people expected God to orchestrate this mass emigration is a complex topic that deals with the irrational and prayer, but the direct appeal to God regarding this matter ought to make sense from a purely theological perspective. The land of Israel is the Promised Land, that is, a land promised to the Jewish people as recorded in the Torah: "On that day the Lord made a covenant with Abram, saying, 'To your descendants I give this land, from the river of Egypt to the great river, the river Euphrates.'"[66] According to this verse, God not only promises Israel to Abraham's children, which includes the Children of Israel or the Jewish people, but describes the borders of the Promised Land expansively, reaching as far south as the Nile in Egypt and as far north as the Euphrates in present day Iraq. Such a country would encompass all of present day Israel and sections of present day Egypt, Lebanon, and Syria. That's a serious piece of real estate. The Book of Numbers (chapter 34) also has God describing the borders of Israel, but these boundaries are far more modest. The United

------

66   Genesis 15:18

Nations Partition Plan of 1947, which divided the land among Jews and Arabs, created a Jewish homeland that did not correspond with either of the two biblical narratives. In sum, *Eretz Yisra'el*, the Land of Israel, is an amorphous piece of geography, expanding and shrinking over time, its borders determined by a host of political and military consequences. But the inability to determine the exact footprint of this Promised Land is irrelevant to the fact that there is an historic and spiritual connection between the Jewish people and ... not Uganda, considered at one time as a possible Jewish homeland; not New Jersey, which in the early 1900's developed a Zionist commune; not the North Pole, where some segment of the world would like to send Jews, as if that would end anti-Semitism (It wouldn't). The Jewish people's historic and spiritual connection with geography is with that piece of Middle Eastern land that one may drive through, north to south, in a single day. This is the Jewish homeland that history, politics, religion and war have carved out for the Jews, and the idea that all this materialized just a few years after 6,000,000 Jews were murdered is a true to life miracle, a phoenix rising from the ashes. The significance of May 14, 1948, the day Israel became a sovereign Jewish state, cannot be underestimated. There is no nation without a plot of land to call its own. That Jews somehow managed to retain a sense of Jewish nationhood for 1900 years, though they were landless, is remarkable.

The absurdity of a people without a land was a major bugaboo in welcoming Jews as equals within the modern world.

Jews were forever suspected of playing the fifth column, the people who say they are citizens and true patriots when in fact they remain connected to some fantasy country, one destroyed long ago, but one that they would readily return to should fate afford the opportunity. "Could the Jews be trusted?" was a question that modern states championing equality had to ask. Because Jews made no secret of their longing to return to their ancient homeland, trust in Jews as equals would be contingent on purging them of their sense of nationhood.

One example of a Christian majority struggling with the idea of social parity with Jews is curiously found in French Revolutionary history. Napoleon Bonaparte (1769-1821), the great French military leader and emperor, had lifted various bans on the Jews in France, Germany, and Italy, which had kept them isolated from the mainstream and maintained them as second-class citizens. In April 1806, Napoleon convened an Assembly of Jewish Notables who were to answer twelve questions bearing on the relationship between Jews, their non-Jewish neighbors, and the secular state. For example, one question dealt with the French—do Jews see them as fellow citizens or strangers? Another question dealt with intermarriage—may Jews marry Christians or not? The assembly was headed by the respected French Talmudist, Rabbi Joseph David Sinzheim of Strasbourg (1745-1812). As an Orthodox Jew, these questions were deeply troubling, but he and his associates managed to come up with answers that satisfied the emperor. In order to transform the answers into law, and in order to be sure that Jews throughout Europe—at least that vast section of Europe now under French rule—would accept the answers as law, a new Sanhedrin, the ancient ruling institution of the Jewish people, was to be reconstituted. Jewish delegates from across Europe were invited to compose this seventy-one-member pseudo-legislative body. This institution established by Napoleon first met in February of 1807, and is known today as the Grand Sanhedrin.

Question number six pertained to Jews and nationhood. Do Jews born in France regard France as their country? Are they obligated to fight for this country and abide by the laws of its civil codes? These questions would resolve, once and for all, whether Jews would be true to the land of their birth or true to some remembered nation destroyed long ago. Rabbi Sinzheim and associates assured Napoleon that Jews were French, that they were obligated to defend and fight for France, and that they were bound to follow French law as would any French citizen. The Grand Sanhedrin ratified that position and thus the contemporary Jew was born—a Jew for whom religious tradition and nationhood were suddenly divided one from the other. From now on, Judaism would be a religion, but Jews themselves would not constitute a nation, even one in exile.

Rabbi Samuel Holdheim, a leading figure in German Reform Judaism, said it quite plainly at the Reform rabbinic conference of 1845: "The hope for a national restoration contradicts our feeling for the Fatherland."[67] Certainly, all good

---

67   Jon Bloomberg, *The Jewish World in the Modern Age* (Ktav, 2004), p. 112.

Jews would want their fidelity to the Fatherland to be beyond question. The saddest and most ironic manifestation of Jews isolated from their ancient, national roots was the slogan of German Reform Judaism: "Berlin is the new Jerusalem."[68] The rupture between religion and nationhood was a division forced upon Jews, and the price paid for entry into modernity.

This modernity-manufactured division is one that confuses Jews to this day. The most vocal contemporary anti-Israel forces rush to remind the public that they are not anti-Semitic, they are only anti-Zionist. Some Jews might even accept that argument as a legitimate distinction. But an examination of that position will expose a more vicious politics. The position seeks to rip Zionism, the Jewish nationalistic movement to restore Jews to their ancestral homeland, from Jewish religious sentiments. But Zionism and Jewish spirituality have been intertwined for centuries, certainly ever since the destruction of the second Temple (70 CE), if not before. Even after Napoleon's Grand Sanhedrin, many Jews continued to pray for a return to Zion, a rebuilt Jerusalem, a Davidic kingdom, and the various institutions that would resurrect the Jewish autonomy of an erstwhile age. So to be anti-Zionist is really to deny Jewish nationhood, and when Jewish nationhood is challenged, Jewish self-determination is repudiated. A landless Jew is a powerless Jew. And there exists a substantial portion of the world that would like to see Jews both defenseless and declawed. For them, the only good Jew is an impotent Jew. As such,

---

68   Kavon, Eli. *http://www.jpost.com/Opinion/Berlin-Jerusalem-and-dual-loyalty-413130*, The Jerusalem Post, August 24, 2015. Accessed: February 25, 2018.

anti-Zionism is anti-Semitic. Anti-Zionism denies Jews the very essence of who a Jew has always been from the beginning—a member of the nation of Israel, *Am Yisra'el.*

This may explain why Jewish law or Halakhah defines a Jew not by any kind of religious litmus test, but only by an accident of birth. According to Halakhah, the one defining feature of a Jew is that one has a Jewish mother or converted to Judaism. One who works ten hours on the Sabbath, breaks for thirty minutes to eat a ham and cheese sandwich, returns home where the living room is graced with a Christmas tree, and says good-night by praying to four gods, or for that matter, no gods, is still a Jew. Why? It is because Jews may have spawned a profound religious tradition, of which we are very proud, but we began as a nation like any other nation, diverse and multifaceted, and not even necessarily all on the same page about one God.

The Bible records any number of episodes in which the people of Israel or the leadership slip into polytheistic beliefs or practices. That's history. The Jewish people have not forgotten their own shortcomings or the complexities of nationhood. And any nation that is worthy of nationhood is an entity of extraordinary diversity and creativity, moments of triumph as well as shame. A nation is organic heterogeneity, bound by all sorts of commonalities—history, language, literature, custom, music, mythologies, and yes, ritual behaviors as well—but nonetheless multifarious. From our earliest writings of what it means to be a Jew, we have thought of ourselves as a nation.

God's initial communication with Abram states just that: "I will make of you a great nation, and I will bless you..."[69] The Hebrew term for nation is *goy,* the very same term used for identifying all the other "nations" in the Bible, whether the Ammonites, Hittites, or Egyptians. And like any other nation in the world, Jews need a government, and that too is something that May 14, 1948 recreated. On that important date, *Am Yisra'el,* the people of Israel, finally reinstituted *Medinat Yisra'el,* the State of Israel.

Medinat Yisra'el is a political entity, a military power, a democratic enterprise, and above all, a Jewish state. On July 5, 1950, the state established the *hok hashevut,* the Law of Return, meaning that Jews who sought to come back to their ancestral homeland could do so with relative ease. Iraqi, Yemini, Syrian, Lebanese, German, Austrian, Polish, Italian, Hungarian, French, and English Jews were drawn to Israel where they could speak the *lingua franca*, the reborn Hebrew language, purchase food in kosher markets, observe Jewish holidays that were now national holidays, and serve in an army to protect the nascent state from constant challenges and real threats to its existence. Today, Israel has succeeded in growing its economy, advancing in technology and medical research, and creating the conditions for artists who paint, sing, sculpt, write, dance, and act— all with a Jewish accent. It is breathtaking. And while there is no downside to the rebirth and growth of this sovereign Jewish nation, *Medinat Yisra'el* is far from a utopia.

---

69   Genesis 12:2

My wife and I took our children to Israel a few times in the 1980's and '90's, and on one such occasion, my daughter, who was about 8 years old, began to cry as we walked to the Western Wall in Jerusalem. Her tears took me by surprise. What was the problem? Beggars. Poor people who were dressed in *shmatas* and nervy in approaching us with their requests. It was the beggars that set her off. As she later explained, she had been taught that Jerusalem was the perfect city. How could there be poor people in the perfect city? That moment pointed to the weakness of the Israel curriculum in the American Jewish school system. Israel was portrayed as perfect, a place where all Jews could live as Jews without fear of the problems that beset them elsewhere.

For years, Jewish educators portrayed Israel as a miracle and a utopian state for Jews. A miracle it was. A utopia? Not so much. The Jews from Arab States, so often poor both financially and professionally, found themselves shunned by the more educated and western Ashkenazic Jews of European origin. Survivors of the Holocaust did not always find an outstretched and welcoming hand. Stories of young Israelis taunting survivors, calling them *"sabon"* or soap, are unconscionable but true. The horrors of the European Jewish experience reminded tough Israelis of the powerless, helpless Diaspora Jews, a stereotype the Israelis were actively suppressing. Among people that had too often experienced the effects of bigotry and prejudice were too many people who themselves espoused bigoted and prejudiced views against their Arab neighbors.

The ultra-Orthodox had worked out an arrangement with the government whereby they were not only exempt from military duty, but received substantial stipends from the government to do little more than study in their own *yeshivot.* Among the toughest aspects of Israeli life for the majority of American Jews was and continues to be the political clout given to the Chief Rabbinate of Israel, an ultra-Orthodox and intolerant clerical association. This group has denied everyone but themselves the right to convert non-Jews to Judaism. The Chief Rabbinate denies liberal Jewish rabbis the right to officiate at marriages. Israel's ultra-Orthodox political parties have turned the Western Wall, a shrine that ought to be a symbol of international Jewish solidarity, into an Orthodox synagogue. It's all very frustrating, and for many liberal Israelis, infuriating.

Much of the debate around Israel has to do with the legitimacy or illegitimacy of Diaspora Jewry criticizing Israel. Is it right for people who do not face the daily threats that Israelis do, who do not pay Israeli taxes, who have no commitment to serve in Israel's military, to criticize Israel at all? Perhaps the role of Diaspora Jewry is simply to support the State of Israel, right or wrong. While many Jews think this way, there are an equal number if not more who do not.

The idea that a Jew should remain silent in light of an Israeli government that may be moving in the wrong direction can be interpreted as a violation of Jewish law and principles. "You shall not hate your kinsfolk in your heart. Reprove your kinsman but incur no guilt because of him."[70] This verse actually establishes criticism as a *mitzvah,* a divine command, but Jewish tradition evolved to permit only "kosher criticism," that is criticism offered only under certain conditions. First and foremost, the criticism must be offered lovingly. This is a case in which style is as important as substance. If one screams, the only thing communicated will be anger. Speak softly and calmly, and the criticism just may be heard. The fact is that a great deal of criticism of Israel is not offered lovingly. Second, the criticized must be open to receiving the reproof. Governments vary as to how open they are to criticism. As for those which are resistant to or actively crush criticism, they paradoxically create the very conditions for further and sharper criticism.

All this should be taken in light of the ancient sage Hillel's dictum: "Do not judge anyone until you have arrived in their place."[71] As close as the alliance is between America and Israel, each resides in very different neighborhoods. America may worry about nuclear threats from Iran (Tehran to New York: 6120 miles) or North Korea (Pyongyang to New York: 6783 miles), but not from its closest neighbors, Mexico or Canada. Israel, in contrast, must worry about nuclear threats from Iran (Tehran to Tel Aviv: 1927 miles) and any number of crude missiles from Gaza (Gaza City to Tel Aviv: 44 miles). Israel's proximity to threat skews the politics to the right. It would be difficult to fully appreciate the anxiety without living in Israel

---

70   Leviticus 19:17

71   Pirkei Avot 2:5

itself. There is a naïve notion that filters through Western minds that if only people would sit down with their opponents and work out the details, peace could be achieved. When deliberations are conducted in good faith, solutions will be found. When problems like the elusiveness of Middle Eastern peace persist, it is because of a deficit of good faith. These days, the accusations for that lack of good faith target the Israeli government itself. This accusation, when emanating from the United States, is ironic in the extreme. Given the political polarization within American society, fellow citizens have found it all but impossible to compromise, yet the expectation that Israel make peace with enemies sworn to its destruction persists as reasonable. Maybe American Jews expect more of Israelis than they do of themselves.

If the existential threats to the Jewish state seem isolated from the way Israel dismisses the values of the liberal Jewish communities, it may be because the present Israeli government, in coalition with ultra-Orthodox parties, needs to accommodate those parties in order to maintain the coalition and thus its power. In other words, the opposition to the liberal Jewish communities does not necessarily stem from a philosophical objection, but only political calculation. The political anxiety is as great as the perceived existential threat. The two terrorist organizations with which Israel must contend, Hezbollah in the North and Hamas in the South, are both committed to Israel's destruction. To the extent that each sees Israel as diabolic, as evil through and through, logic in their estimation would not call for compromise, but for destruction of the state. In fact, that is their goal, which they have made clear. There are abundant historical examples that would suggest that threats of this nature should be taken at face value. In this way we can understand how the principal powers in Israel would do nothing to upset the delicate balance of its coalition, for fear that control may be ceded to a leadership of lesser vigilance.

Of course, one of the criticisms of Israel is that it may be taking advantage of the Arab threat, exaggerating it to their own end in order to avoid negotiations that might lead to further territorial concessions. This point is worthy of discussion and debate. But in the end, the government of Israel is a democratically-elected government and will do what needs to be done from its own subjective perspective. Imperfect? Without question. But such imperfection must be placed in context: there is no perfect government anywhere on earth. There never has been. There never will be. And here is the truth: That state of perfection, like the messiah, like God picking up the Jewish people and leading them by hand back to the Promised Land, is sheer fantasy. To maintain a state and an army will repeatedly present the state with moral and ethical dilemmas for which the only response may be between options that are individually horrible, stupid, unethical, or unconscionable. All states face dilemmas of this nature, as do individuals, with the intent to hopefully choose the least damaging of the available options. In a world that has grown as polarized and radical as ours, in a neighborhood as tough as the Mideast, the State of Israel has learned that there is great wisdom in speaking with the voice of Jacob, as long as one makes known that it is prepared to use the hands of Esau.

Jews, as people who live with a God-consciousness, dare not divorce themselves from the plight of the Palestinians or Arab neighbors who surround Israel. They are as deserving of peace and prosperity as all others who reside on earth. The miserable conditions to which they are subject are sadly due, in no small measure, to a leadership that would sooner focus on Israel's destruction than its own national interest. The nature of a people's governance has far-reaching consequences for the people subject to its rule. And where it is possible to compel such changes that would benefit the Palestinian people, Jews should be at the forefront of that change. But damning Israel with the expectation that this will in some way help the Palestinians is an illusion of all those who think that change must primarily come from without and not from within. No successful person subscribes to such a formula. So Jews who divorce themselves from the State of Israel in protest for all they see as unjust, in the end, help no one. To the contrary, they are the success stories of every anti-Semitic movement that ever existed, that would want to see Jews isolated from their homeland, powerless, assimilated beyond recognition, and invisible.

Jews may never divorce themselves from Israel. Even if we are not citizens of the State of Israel, we are always members of the People of Israel, who always have a connection to the land of Israel. The land teaches that we are of the same provenance; the people urges that as family, we must love one another; and the state assures that the Jewish people have a home, and that there is a price to pay for anyone who spills Jewish blood.

• • • • •

TO THE ZIONISM SKEPTIC

You're right—Israel is not a utopia and is dealing with many problems, the effects of which we all may feel. But the State of Israel is, nevertheless, one of the great Jewish miracles of the twentieth and twenty-first century. It is the Jewish home-land and thus our homeland, on some level, as well. If we want to make real change for both Jews and Arabs, the way to do it is to remain connected, not disconnected, to Israel, a political entity that can demonstrate how success is possible for all the people of the Middle East.

13 THE SACRED RITUALS SKEPTIC

*I'm not that religious, but really:
What is the point of Jewish ritual when all
that really matters is whether or not you
are a good person?*

The mikvah or ritual pool is among the most precious institutions within the Jewish community. Though men use the mikvah, it is more closely associated with married women who immerse in it monthly as part of a purification ritual following their menstrual cycle. The immersion allows women to resume intimate relations with their husbands, relations that are temporarily suspended during their period and for sometime thereafter. Because *tzeni'ut* or modesty is so highly valued within the community, immersions typically take place under the cover of night and supervised solely by a woman who has been designated or hired for that purpose. During those evening immersions, men are not allowed in the mikvah. In 2014, Barry Freundel, the rabbi of Kesher Israel Congregation in Washington, DC, was arrested and charged with six counts of voyeurism, which were ultimately connected to him based on a camera installed in the National Capital Mikvah. Jews of all denominations and throughout the world were shocked and outraged. The rabbi's trial ended with him pleading guilty to fifty-two counts of voyeurism. He was fined $13,000 and given a six-and-half year prison sentence.

There is nothing more damaging to Jewish observance or religion in general than people who are purportedly models of sacred behavior who are eventually exposed as criminals. Weren't all those rituals they fulfilled designed to keep them on some path of righteousness? Is it all sanctimony designed to fool the public at large? It is disheartening and leads to the question of whether or not Jewish ritual has any worthwhile function at all, particularly since it would seem that goodness, honesty, and fairness, ought to be given the higher priority.

This sentiment is hardly a modern phenomenon. The prophet Isaiah was furious with those who might engage in pious behaviors at the expense of pursuing the good in life. Commenting on those who would gain favor of God through fasts and holy remonstrations like the wearing of sackcloth and ashes, he wrote:

> Do you call that a fast,
>
> A day acceptable to the Lord?
>
> No, this is the fast I desire:
>
> To unlock the bonds of wickedness,
>
> And untie the cords of the yoke
>
> To let the oppressed go free;

To break off every yoke.

It is to share your bread with the hungry,

And to take the wretched poor into your home;

When you see the naked to cloth him,

And not to hide from your own kin.[72]

Written some 2700 years ago, Isaiah knew that ritual was never in place of the good and that the pursuit of goodness was in fact key to a life of godliness. But that proposition was never meant to have the good replace ritual. Ritual had a role to play in Jewish religious life, just as it had and continues to have in the ethos of every ethnicity and nationality the world over.

The notion that ritual is in some way a throwback to a pre-scientific age, an age of ignorance or superstition, is a huge misunderstanding of ritual and a remarkable incognizance of rituals' functions in everyday life. Ritual is something that marks an occasion and grounds one in the moment. America is full of such rituals like singing the national anthem before a ball game, displaying the American flag on national holidays, or eating turkey on Thanksgiving. These routines are expected and establish connections between members of a group, in this case, members of that special group known as Americans. Rituals also mark transitions, and so there are both morning and evening rituals. For some people, the day would not start properly were it not preceded by a morning shower, a cup of coffee, or a perusal of the headlines, either on the internet or from a bona fide hard copy newspaper. In the evening, bedtime

---

72   Isaiah 58:5b-7

may be preceded by a few minutes of late night TV, or a bowl of ice cream, or kissing one's spouse good night. In developing these personal rituals, people create the routines that help them transition from one period of the day to the next.

It's important to distinguish between a ritual and a superstition. A ritual marks an occasion, grounds one in the moment, binds the members of a particular group together, and eases transition. A superstition, in contrast, is something meant to ward off failure, illness, mishap or death. Baseball players are notoriously famous for such superstitious behaviors. Wade Boggs played professional baseball for eighteen years primarily with the Boston Red Sox. He was a third-baseman, an outstanding hitter, and in 2005 was inducted into the Baseball Hall of Fame. Before every game, he would eat chicken and when he positioned himself in the batter's box, he used his bat to draw the Hebrew word *hai*, meaning life, in the dirt. Boggs is not even Jewish. He did retire with a .328 batting average— very impressive! Was it the chicken or the *hai?* Perhaps it was just due to Boggs being a marvelous athlete. Superstitions may be routine, but they do not qualify as ritual.

Many years ago, a devoted member of the congregation threw his hands up in the air, and shouted, "You're too damn creative." He really caught me off guard and I wasn't sure how to take it. From the parts I hailed from, creativity was, by and large, a good thing. It would be difficult to imagine anyone having too much of it, since much of the world suffers from a deficit, not a surfeit, of creativity. The way he announced the observation did not make it sound like a criticism, nor was it necessarily a compliment, so somewhat confused, I asked for clarification. The man, a college professor, elaborated as follows (I paraphrase here, of course): "Rabbi, my life is a basket of uncertainty and unpredictability. I give lectures without knowing whether my students have prepared or if they appreciate anything I'm saying. It's unclear which colleague will be questioning my most recent research. The dean is forever commenting on my students' complaints. I feel pressed to do things I'd rather not do in order to achieve tenure. I worry constantly whether the future will have me searching for another teaching position, of which few are available, and those that do may take me far from my son (who lives with his mother, my ex) and whom I do not wish to abandon. When I come to synagogue, I just want the service to be as the week before, and next week, I would like the service to be as it was this week. The synagogue is the only place I can come to where I won't be surprised. And since most of the surprises I encounter professionally are unpleasant, I would prefer the assurance of knowing that you're not going to pull a fast one on us, but that everything will be boringly and predictably the same. It's the one stable part of my life that I count on. And as my luck would have it, you wind up my rabbi, one of the most creative people I have ever met, and it's driving me crazy. Could you please just be more boring!"

I never forgot that encounter. In less than sixty seconds, he taught me more about ritual than I had ever learned while at seminary. Because time-honored rituals tend to stay the same for years, they create a sense of stability and permanence. It's comforting.

The High Holidays are a time of year when synagogues around the world are brimming with Jews. And for those Jews whose custom it is to belong to a synagogue, chances are they have their set place within the sanctuary. This is true even for those congregations that have open seating. People tend to drift to the same space where other friends and family have drifted as well. Rabbis who have been with congregations for several years will be able to look at an empty sanctuary and tell you where the Simsons, the Ehrenkranzes, the Kaplans, the Weisses, and all the Warshauers sit. They are there year after year. It's a ritual. And their yearly faithful return to their space creates a sense of stability and permanence, which however illusory, nonetheless comforts and sustains in an unnerving world whose only constant is change.

And then, from time to time, a seat previously occupied by a known character, someone who belongs in that seat, is suddenly empty. Someone has left, someone is ill, someone is no longer with the community, and the vacated space alters the experience of the holiday. Mrs. Tendler, who sat in the middle of the row or Dr. Sadoff who always sat up front in an aisle chair—missing! Their absence is yet another reminder that our lives are neither permanent nor eternal. Everything changes. Nothing stays the same. But when the community responds by regrouping, returning to the other rituals of the holiday, then life goes on with a renewed, albeit a more somber sense of stability.

Jewish rituals mark occasions, establish connections between members of a group, and ease transitions from one moment to the next. There is something else that Jewish rituals do: they compel us to think about what is good in life, what is worthwhile, true, and enduring. A central verse of the Torah is "Remember the Sabbath day and keep it holy."[73] I grew up in a family that took this verse to heart. When I was a teen, one of our family rules was that on Friday nights, the siblings were not permitted to go out to a party or social event. The rule was that the entire family had to be present for Shabbat dinner. There is no question that I resented the rule on occasion, but in general, it did not feel restrictive. It was an effective way to create a Shabbat experience that was integral to the family. Sitting at the dinner table, saying the blessings, and then staying home were the very substance of the evening. During that time, my father was no longer a tailor, my mother no longer a home-maker, my sister no longer a teacher, and my brother and I no longer students. We were not defined by the jobs we fulfilled, but by the familial roles we played. We were just family inter-acting with each other and safeguarded from the powers who made demands of us. Americans, when asked who they are, will often define themselves by what they do: a doctor, a small business owner, an academic, etc. It's a social convention that is at best an evasion, because it says little about who you are.

---

73   Exodus 20:8

There are thousands of doctors, thousands of small business owners, and thousands of academics. Who are you and what do you really do? Shabbat is the day when we may no longer define ourselves by what we do, for it is the day when we not only don't do it, there is reason for us to avoid conversation about business or professional issues. It would not be in the spirit of Shabbat, that is, as is said, *"not Shabbosdik."*

The renowned neurologist, Oliver Sacks (1933-2015), wrote a moving piece in *The New York Times* on the comfort of ritual. Having been raised in an Orthodox Jewish home in England, he was well-versed in the ritual rhythms and customs of the tradition. He recalled with great fondness the observance of Shabbat, with its family dinners, prayers in the synagogue, visits with family, and so forth. As he matured and eventually moved to America, he drifted from it all, and owing to a particularly hurtful encounter with his mother, ended up very much alienated from his traditional roots. But he returned, largely through the friendship and compassion of his cousin, Robert John Aumann, the Nobel laureate in economics, and himself an Orthodox Jew. Through that fortuitous connection, he made a trip to Israel late in his life and experienced once again the beauty of Shabbat observance. At the time he wrote the essay, Sacks was quite ill. He concluded the essay as follows:

> And now, weak, short of breath, my once-firm muscles melted away by cancer, I find my thoughts, increasingly, not on the supernatural or spiritual, but what is meant by living a good and worthwhile

life—achieving a sense of peace within oneself. I find my thoughts drifting to the Sabbath, the day of rest, the seventh day of the week, and perhaps the seventh day of one's life as well, when one can feel that one's work is done, and one may, in good conscience, rest.[74]

Sacks died two weeks later. Judging from this final article, he died peacefully.

When life is reduced to simply doing one's job, and living only between gigs or projects, the risk of an encounter with meaninglessness and malaise increases exponentially. People need more out of life than a task or a responsibility, or as far as that goes, a career or a profession. Sadly, life in the Western liberal world richly provides material blessings to many, but falls woefully short of spiritual satisfactions.

This absence of meaning spills over into all aspects of life, such that no matter what relationship we are in or what task we must fulfill, the question of its meaning or purpose may be sitting anxiously in some corner of our minds. If you are married, you may question whether the marriage is fulfilling. If you are single, you may question whether something is missing. If you are working, you may wonder if your job is commensurate with your talents. And if you are unemployed, or divorced, or childless, you may wonder whether your life is of meaning at all. Humans crave meaning and purposefulness, in whatever it

---

74   *The New York Times*, August 14, 2015

is we do. And when it comes to Jewish ritual, the ritual will be welcomed only if it speaks to us in some deep and compelling manner. Where ritual practice appears rote, habitual or perfunctory, its appeal will suffer, and its purpose will falter. One ritual particularly vulnerable to mechanical fulfillment is prayer.

At the root of the Hebrew word meaning to pray is the three-lettered verb, *pilel,* which means to judge, expect or dream. The verb in Hebrew to pray, however, is *lehitpallel,* a reflexive construction which would literally suggest a judging, expectation or a dreaming of oneself. It is perhaps because we live in a Christian world that we so often think of prayer as a request for something, some blessing or some divine intervention. No doubt, a part of prayer is meant to do just that, but it is not necessarily the paramount function of prayer.

A theology professor once posed the following question to her students: If you wanted to find out what Jews do and how they think, which primary sacred text would you turn to first? Virtually everyone said the Bible. She smiled and said: "No, you would turn to the prayer book." It was for me, as I believe it was for the others in the class, an ah-ha moment. None of us had ever thought of the prayer book as a compendium of Jewish values and beliefs. Having used it solely for the purpose of running through the requisite prayers, and very often having done so at breakneck speed, we had failed to absorb the overall thrust of the prayer book, which was to rehearse within the Jewish mind the values and beliefs that make us who we are. But so what! What meaning is there in gathering together routinely to rehearse what it is we believe in? Isn't the point of prayer to request God's blessings or intervention in our lives? Maybe, but returning again to the Hebrew *lehitpallel,* we find in that verb that Jewish prayer may have as much to do with the pray-er as it does with God.

Prayer doesn't change things. Prayer changes people and people change things.

I love that maxim. It's anonymous, but I wish I could meet the person who wrote it, because whoever did understood prayer better than most. Through the words of the prayer book, we review the fundamental, shared beliefs of an ancient heritage and then face the much harder demand of prayer, that of self-analysis:

> We believe in justice, but are we pursuing justice for those who have been denied it?
>
> We cherish Israel, but are we doing our best to protect Israel?
>
> We love God, but do our interactions with others reflect that love of God?

Are we the best version of who we can be, or are we trapped by the demands and expectations of others who compel us to act as they wish us to be?

Given all this, we should lament the emphasis in Jewish education on getting the Hebrew right, and on getting the tune right, at the expense of getting people to pause and reflect in a moment of *hitpallelut,* prayerfulness, in which the focus is not on what God can do for us, but on what we are meant to do for God and all of God's creations. The most authentic of Jewish prayers may be the one in which the words emanate not from the pages of the prayer book, but from the heart in self-assessment. That is the most genuine *avodah shebalev,* a worship of the heart, as the rabbis referred to prayer. Prayer is much more than pious declarations. Prayer is a strategy for reorienting ourselves, our consciousness and our behaviors, in the pursuit of those values we cherish, that is, in the pursuit of the good.

Although Shabbat and prayer cover a lot of ritual territory in any overview of Jewish tradition, a single chapter cannot possibly be exhaustive of all or even most of Jewish ritual practice. But there is one more fundamental area of Jewish practice that has defined Jews throughout the ages, and to ignore it would be an inexcusable oversight: *kashrut* or the Jewish dietary laws. Of the three primary areas of Jewish ritual practice *kashrut* is the most challenging as it most easily defies rationalization. One can more readily justify a day of rest, and one can understand how people might turn to God in prayer, but what possible issue could God have with anyone eating a cheeseburger or a lobster roll? The rabbis, too, understood this issue in describing *kashrut* as a <u>h</u>ok, that is, a law which rests on no rational foundation. Indeed, the argument has been made that as such, *kashrut* is critical to the faith of the Jew for one who observes it can observe it only in deference to God's authority without recourse to any rational justification. It is truly an act of obedience before God. Well, maybe, but a cursory survey of the Jewish community would uncover any number of atheists who keep kosher, and they certainly can't be doing it for God.

One of the ironies of *kashrut* is that long after Jews distanced themselves from daily prayer, and no longer observed Shabbat rigorously, many remained committed to the dietary laws. The arational had a firmer grip upon them than the rational. For those who see meaning in maintaining a ritual simply because one's parents did so as did one's grandparents, a more rational explanation of the ritual would be unnecessary. There is substantial integrity in maintaining a tradition on that basis. The question is may such a justification languish in an age where change is the constant, or would it prevail precisely because change is the constant and some countervailing force needed? We will leave any answers to the professional augurs, but pursue some line of reasoning to justify the dietary laws.

In the section of Torah that deals extensively with forbidden and permitted foods,[75] there is what might be regarded as a rationalization for *kashrut*:

> For I the Lord am your God: you shall sanctify yourselves and be holy, for I am holy. You shall not defile yourselves through any swarming thing that crawls upon the earth. For I am the Lord who brought you up from the land of Egypt to be your God: you shall therefore be holy, for I am holy.[76]

---

75   See Leviticus 11

76   Leviticus 11:44-45

This rationalization may be a concern that "any swarming thing," a generalized term for that which is not kosher, may be unclean and thus to be avoided, an argument that moderns will most likely take exception to. Plenty of people the world over eat swarming things without negative consequence. The rationalization also suggests a you-owe-Me argument, that is, because I (i.e., God) took you out of Egypt, you must now fulfill this demand, no matter how arbitrary it may sound. This also may strike moderns odd, for why would God be portrayed as demanding something so arbitrary as *kashrut?* It is an unwitting characterization of God as fickle. Finally, recalling the idea that the *kadosh* or holy is that which is separate or distinct, *kashrut* may be just that system that creates a distinct gastronomy for Jews, rendering them holy through a unique set of eating habits. *Kashrut* has functioned in that way throughout the generations. One needn't have a specific reason to keep kosher other than it was the Jewish thing to do. This would satisfy *kashrut* as a ritual designed to bind a people together. Moreover, it is no more or less arational than singing the national anthem before a ball game. Still, moderns might crave a reason for *kashrut* more compelling than—it's what Jews do.

I agree that *kashrut* has something to do with the sacred, not in the sense of distinct, but rather as that which must be left undisturbed. So, for example, there were certain parts of the ancient Temple that were off-limits to regular Jews (i.e., non-priests or Levites), precisely because it was a precinct too holy for them to enter. There are times during the year when it is forbidden to work, to go about our business as usual, because the time is sacred and not to be sullied by mundane activity. And finally, there are aspects of the earth that are to remain untouched, because "the earth is the Lord's and all that it holds."[77] We are guests on God's planet Earth. All guests know that when in another's home, we are not free to roam throughout the house without permission and we certainly are not welcome to open any drawers at will. We are guests and there are areas of the house which are off limits to us. Earth is our temporary home and we are mere guests. We must conduct ourselves accordingly, preserving its resources and letting the wild things live, because so far we have found no other home among the approximately 100 billion stars in our Milky Way galaxy. *Kashrut* teaches forbearance, and where others might thoughtlessly or even happily exploit the earth's gifts, we should not be so brazen as to think these resources unlimited, for all economics and ecology teaches just the opposite: the rude reality of limited and finite resources.

My rabbi, Kassel Abelson, rabbi emeritus of Beth El Synagogue in St. Louis Park, MN, offered an insightful take on *kashrut*. Responding to a question about the purpose of *kashrut* and its relevance to modern life, he said (and I paraphrase): "If you can get people to think *seriously* about the ethics of eating a cheeseburger, just think what moral constraints that imposes on they who might be inclined to cheat a customer, lie in court, or doctor up a tax return." Of course, the sobering

---

77   Psalm 24:1

reality is that there have been plenty of well-documented glatt kosher eating Jews who fail to rise to an acceptable moral standard. Then again, Rabbi Abelson's point pivoted on the word *seriously,* that is, imagine the Jewish world if it were to think deeper about *kashrut* and its implications, rather than just as a thing that Jews do. Jesus is famously recorded as saying, "It is not what goes into the mouth that defiles a person, but what comes out of the mouth that defiles a person."[78] He made a good point, but the modern world has found a hundred different reasons why people should think carefully about what goes into their mouths. The Jewish people have been ahead of the curve for centuries, though their reasons were for ethical, not physical results. Their commitment to *kashrut* has been one of the defining attributes of Jewish ritual life. It is yet another ritual that binds Jews through the ages, past and future, and over borders, throughout the world. Many claim that the observance of *kashrut* has nothing to do with ethics, but the very fact that *kashrut* also binds Jews to a God consciousness is a fundamental basis for delimiting the authentic Jewish life to one that is also an ethical life.

To hear most people talk about the good is a curious matter because they tend to speak as if everyone is in agreement as to what the good actually is. The truth of the matter is that over the whole of human history, millions of thought hours and a whole lot of ink has been spilled over the issue of exactly how to determine what is good and what isn't. From the ancient

---

78   Matthew 15:11

Greeks to contemporary thinkers, there are as many answers to the question of what is good as there are the number of times the question has been asked. Joseph Addison (1672-1719), the English essayist and politician, thought that the greatest good was music. That's a definition that I suspect few people on the street would voice. Edmund Burke (1729-1797), the Irish author and orator, thought that organization or order was the greatest good. Many authoritarians would agree with him. When we think about good people, we tend to think about those saintly figures who have sacrificed their lives or devoted their lives toward some greater end. But the surf of history has cast upon the shore any number of murderous wretches who have done the same. Sacrifice may be noble, unless one is making sacrifices toward some evil end. In 2000, Robert A. Rockaway published a book, *But He Was Good to His Mother: The Lives and Crimes of Jewish Gangsters*. The title is based on an observation often voiced within the Jewish community in regard to the Jewish men (they were mostly all men) who stole, lied, and murdered for material gain. "But," one might counter after a listing of crimes committed, "he was good to his mother." Does being good to one's mother absolve one of all the other transgressions? Does it make one "good"?

People may think that defining the good is a no-brainer, but the fact is that facile definitions of the good will typically yield a definition that is sloppy and woefully insufficient. The prayer book answers the question of goodness, with the wisdom of a thousand generations. Shabbat is a powerful antidote to the illusion that our lives are worthwhile to the extent that we produce. *Kashrut* is a reminder to us that we live in a world of limited resources and we ought to moderate our behavior accordingly.

"I'm not that religious," Jews are wont to say. If rabbis were confessors, this would be the most prevalent of all Jewish confessions. What Jews are really saying is that they are uncomfortable with rituals that they do not understand, or have never practiced, or are self-conscious that they may do wrong. They may see a ritual as superstitious or part of a world that is no more. They may even disparage ritual in general, without realizing that everyone, themselves included, engages in rituals daily. Can't we just do good and dispense with all these pesky Jewish rituals? I wish we could, but it isn't a healthy prescription for the future of Judaism or the future of the good.

A rabbinic colleague told me of an experience with a group of congregants that he took to Israel. Their itinerary included a Shabbat stay at a kibbutz that followed Jewish tradition fairly rigorously. It was to be an experience that allowed for interaction with kibbutznicks in a place where the group would have no worries about kosher food or attending a worship service if any were so inclined. What the rabbi and fellow-travelers had not counted on were limitations on their own practice in conformity with the religious sensitivities of the kibbutz. And so the group was asked to refrain from use of cell phones, writing, or the turning on and off of lights, or for that matter, use of most electrical items like hair dryers, shavers, etc., for the duration of Shabbat. Some within the group protested. What right had the kibbutz to infringe on the freedoms of its guests? But such were the rules of the kibbutz, there was no way to alter the itinerary, and the sun was sinking, counting down the minutes remaining before Shabbat. My colleague, praying for the wisdom of Solomon, offered the following challenge to the group (and I again paraphrase): "Look, here we are, and there is no time to make any changes to our itinerary. We are about to experience a Shabbat in a way that many of us have never experienced it. In the privacy of your own rooms, you may do as you please, but in any public setting, we are going to have to abide by the customs of our hosts, as any guests would. Given the circumstances, some of you might consider an experiment in refraining from writing, and using your cell phone and electrical appliances for all of Shabbat, both publicly and privately. We are only talking twenty-five hours and it may just be the sort of experience that transforms the way you think and feel about a traditional Shabbat observance."

"So did anyone take you up on it?" I asked.

"They all became Sabbath-observers in public for the day, and a few told me that they took up the challenge in private as well."

"And," I asked, "did it change anyone's practice?"

"No," he replied, "but the group remembers the experience as one of the highlights of the trip and as one of my members who observed Shabbat kibbutz-style both publicly and privately put it: 'I'm not that religious, Rabbi, but the whole experience was far more meaningful than I thought it would be, and it made me feel a lot more Jewish.'"

• • • • •

TO THE SACRED RITUALS SKEPTIC

Jewish ritual, fulfilled mindfully, links us to Jewish commu-nity, past, present and future, to the Bible, to God, and estab-lishes an ethical direction to our lives in a modern world that has failed to create purpose and meaning in the lives of its constituents.

EPILOGUE

One of my best friends growing up in Minneapolis was a kid by the name of Abe Chames. My small group of bright, athletically-challenged, and relatively unpopular pre-pubescents knew him as Abey. He had a cherubic face and a delightful laugh that would make everyone around him laugh, even when nothing was particularly funny. Our playtime consisted of riding our bikes, though Abey's mother wouldn't let him ride much further than the block on which the family lived. Somehow we found time to venture a few blocks down the way to a corner drugstore where we could pick up pop (known as soda in other parts of the country), Snickers bars, the latest issue of MAD magazine, and then get back to Abey's block before his mother knew we had strayed. We talked about school, characters in the neighborhood, girls with cooties, and oddly enough, even at ten or eleven years of age, we talked religion. Abey's family belonged to an Orthodox synagogue while our family, at the time, belonged to Mikro Kodesh, a "traditional synagogue." In the Midwest, a traditional synagogue would be a place with an Orthodox liturgy but a space where men and women could sit together. Our religious differences were hardly pronounced, and as we reflected on the respective attributes of the synagogues we attended, discussion focused largely on the food served at the *kiddush* and the relative accents of the rabbis' English. Over time, the two of us went our separate ways but were destined to meet again in New York City, where Abey was finishing his studies at the Orthodox Yeshiva University and I at the Conservative Jewish Theological Seminary. We met at the Lower East Side's Schmulka Bernstein's, a well-known glatt kosher Chinese deli, for dinner and catching-up.

We were delighted to see each other again and reminisced on times past. The conversation eventually turned to our views of theology, Torah, and Halakhah. Abey's views on all these matters were deeply traditional. God had written the Torah; Jewish law was the word of God even when interpreted by the rabbis, and none of it was subject to change. After four years of college and five years at the Seminary, my own views on these matters had evolved substantially. God had influenced people to write Torah, but the Torah itself was a human production. Nevertheless, in a world marred by sin and failure, these human authors were spiritually astute and keenly perceptive of God's presence in the world. They were artists of the spirit and had directed us all onto a path of righteousness via laws and traditions. Moreover, the rabbis, throughout time, knew what changes needed to be made in order to keep Jewish law fresh and alive so that it always spoke directly to the Jewish people.

At that point, Abey said something that has stuck with me for a long time. In a rather wistful manner he said, "You know, your faith is greater than mine."

"What?"

"Yes, your faith is greater than mine. I just can't conceive of mankind producing Torah. But you can. In order for Torah to do what it does, I need to believe in a superpower who is in total control. But you actually think that humans have accomplished this. Your faith is far greater than mine."

His observation surprised me. In truth, it shocked me. My college and seminary years had thrust a thousand secularized ideas into my head, and as such, I had perceived myself as having salvaged a faith rather than having delved into one. I had reconstructed a faith far more attenuated than the one I had been raised in, or so I assumed. I had grown a bit more skeptical of God's direct role in human affairs and reassigned God to a much more nuanced involvement. My presumption was that in having drifted from the traditional faith, I had come to a different kind of faith, and such a faith could not possibly be stronger than the one with which I was raised. But perhaps Abey's observation was correct. Perhaps the idea that faith that makes room for skepticism is damaged was simply the unconscious bias of my traditional upbringing at work.

The real issue at hand had to do with the nature of questioning faith itself. The conventional wisdom would conceive of faith as some set of principles or beliefs which were unassailable. To question any one of those beliefs would thus be an attack on faith itself, the consequence of which would be either a dismantling of faith as a whole or in the very least a substantial portion of it. The implication of such a conception is that faith can only deteriorate but never evolve. Once an accepted principle is questioned, faith is destabilized, and any further questioning could only further jolt an enterprise already teetering on total collapse. But suppose faith was not a static set of beliefs. Suppose, instead, faith was an organic set of beliefs that evolves as humans gain deeper insights into the nature of life. In such a scheme, skepticism itself could lead to a distilling rather than a dismantling of faith. Much of course would depend on the intent of the skepticism. If the intent was to discredit religious tradition, then such skepticism would undoubtedly lead to just that. But if the skepticism was an effort to reconcile conflicting truths within a world that one understands as the handiwork of God, then skepticism would be an essential tool in the refining of faith. Mel, the man who questioned the *Yigdal* prayer as related in the Introduction, raised doubts not to incriminate faith but to come upon a faith with greater integrity, a faith that spoke to him and which he therefore could speak—really sing!—about, with some degree of credibility.

A couple of points about questioning itself may be helpful toward further understanding its essential role in creating a contemporary faith. First, the rabbinic literature is full of questions. If questions were removed from the sacred literature, little would be left. As far as that goes, disagreement among the rabbis is found on almost every page of the Talmudic literature. Those disagreements are recorded for posterity to teach subsequent generations that they will never be the first to come to conflicting answers to the many questions that abound. One need only consider the example of the Haggadah, the text that guides the Passover seder, as proof of the importance of questions. Four questions are asked at the beginning of the Haggadah. And the answers? They are not immediately presented. Better that the assembled answer those questions themselves. Maybe the participants will come up with some unique answers to the questions. And maybe not. But the point is that the answers need not be immediately identified in a culture that places a greater premium on questioning itself.

Second is an idea that I am fond of repeating: there is no such thing as a dumb question. I don't mean this as a Pollyannaish appraisal of questions in general or patronization of the Jewish people. And just for the record, I don't believe the same is true of answers or responses to those questions. In that case, there exists an abundance of hedging, evasive, incomplete, apologetic, unconvincing, and downright stupid answers. But questions, like fruits and vegetables, are essentially always kosher. That is because questioning is evidence of struggle, and struggle defines the essence of what it means to be a Jew. There was a reason why the angel of the Lord changed Jacob's name to *Yisra'el*—one who wrestles with both men and God and prevails. As such, skeptics act as stimulants for growth. In questioning faith, in forcing all of us to rethink, delve into, and ponder our faith, we grow stronger in our faith. "No pain, no gain" may be as true theologically as it is physiologically.

True believers are thinkers. They are unafraid of listening to skeptics and unashamed to admit to personal doubts. To be sure, there are people of faith who shun such questioning and oppose any wavering from the conventional, but rigidity of that nature may actually belie a faith that itself rests on shaky grounds. Permitting no questions nor allowing for doubt may just be a stratagem to protect a faith unable to withstand the scrutiny. And where that is the case, it is possibly due to a faith that is itself flawed, perhaps deeply so, and in need of an overhaul.

An apocryphal story. Once a rabbi and her student got onto an elevator. They needed to go to their classroom on the fifth floor. The elevator rose to the second, the third, the fourth floor and then stopped suddenly. The lights went dark, and the silence suggested a total power failure. The rabbi and her student, trapped in the elevator, heard the voice of an evil spirit: "Choose as you wish—to believe all or deny all things. These are your only choices." The rabbi and student looked at each other blankly for a minute and then the rabbi shouted, "We will believe everything!" The voice of the evil spirit shouted triumphantly, "Stupid, gullible, people!" The lights turned on and the elevator rose to the fifth floor. As the doors opened and they walked out, the student said, "Rabbi, if we believe everything, we then truly are gullible! Our faith will be meaningless." The rabbi responded, "If we deny everything, we deny the truth as well. But if we believe everything, we will also believe the truth. We can only pray that the truth will save us from the deceit and falsehood that pervades the world."

Yigdal Elohim hai are the first three words in the hymn that concludes the Friday night service, meaning "Great is the living God." In this context, we may understand God as all that we regard as true. God is living because the search for truth is a sacred pursuit which is unending and defines the essence of a godly life. The believers of this world have much to teach us about truth. And thank God for the skeptics who want to believe, but who want to believe with a faith that is believable. God is great because God makes for the power of hope and perseverance in a world that all too often may derail and depress us. But God urges us, in spite of everything, to have faith. And if that faith makes room for questions and doubts, not to worry, that is not a compromised faith. Like God, we too are alive and thinking, and to be wholly human is, in part, to be free to question and wonder. So even if we can no longer believe with perfect faith, whatever that means, our expanded or fuller faith, one that allows for skepticism, will do quite well, and may be the only honest faith that there is.